PALE & *Interesting*

# PALE & *Interesting*

decorating with whites, pastels and
neutrals for a warm and welcoming home

ATLANTA BARTLETT
& DAVE COOTE

photography by POLLY WREFORD

RYLAND PETERS & SMALL
LONDON • NEW YORK

**SENIOR DESIGNER** Toni Kay
**COMMISSIONING EDITOR** Annabel Morgan
**LOCATION RESEARCH** Jess Walton
**PRODUCTION** Gordana Simakovic
**ART DIRECTOR** Leslie Harrington
**PUBLISHING DIRECTOR** Alison Starling

*For our beautiful boys.*

First published in 2011.
This revised edition published 2017 by
Ryland Peters & Small
20–21 Jockey's Fields
London WC1R 4BW
*and*
341 E 116th Street
New York, NY 10029
www.rylandpeters.com

10 9 8 7 6 5 4 3 2 1

Text © Atlanta Bartlett & Dave Coote 2011, 2017
Design and photographs
© Ryland Peters & Small 2011, 2017

ISBN: 978-1-84975-854-3

A CIP record for this book is
available from the British Library.

Printed and bound in China

Library of Congress Cataloging-in-Publication data for
the original edition of this book is as follows:

Bartlett, Atlanta.
  Pale & interesting : decorating with whites, pastels,
and neutrals for a warm and welcoming home /
Atlanta Bartlett & Dave Coote ; photography by Polly
Wreford. -- 1st ed.
    p. cm.
  Includes index.
  ISBN 978-1-84975-112-4
  1. Color in interior decoration. 2. White in interior
decoration. I. Coote, Dave. II. Wreford, Polly. III. Title. IV.
Title: Pale and interesting. V. Title: Decorating with
whites, pastels, and neutrals for a warm and
welcoming home.
  NK2115.5.C6B377 2011
  747'.94--dc22
                                          2010049058

# *contents*

# introduction

*Pale & Interesting* is an expression of our design philosophy. It is about putting together a relaxed and comfortable home that reflects your own particular lifestyle and personality; where fashions and trends are noted but not followed rigorously, where good design is essential and the quest to create a happy home – not a show home – is paramount.

This approach to interior design is something that has evolved over the years that we have spent living and working together. When we met, we were both searching for a simpler, more laid-back approach to decorating and, although our styles were quite different – Dave's quite rugged and masculine, and Atlanta's more feminine and predominantly white. What we had in common was a relaxed, simplistic attitude to interior design and a passion for anything old or antique. Over the years honest materials, artful recycling and choosing vintage over newly made and handmade instead of mass-produced became the essence of our look. This progression of ideas culminated in the opening of our mail-order company and online boutique, Pale & Interesting. In this book, we show you how to recreate our easy-going style but, more importantly, we hope we also show you how to tap into your own taste to create a light, airy home that really works for you.

PALE & INTERESTING

GET BACK TO BASICS AND CREATE A HOME THAT CELEBRATES THE SIMPLE THINGS IN
LIFE. EDIT YOUR POSSESSIONS AND ONLY RETAIN WHAT IS USEFUL OR BEAUTIFUL, AND
YOU CAN ENJOY AN ENVIRONMENT THAT IS CALM, EASY AND UNPRETENTIOUS.

*keep it*
*simple*

**OPPOSITE PAGE** An all-white palette and a large skylight make this bright and airy hallway the essence of simplicity. The wood-clad walls, clean lines and lofty proportions contrast beautifully with the quirky features of the original railway carriages around which this house was built.

**THIS PAGE** Less is definitely more in this elegant townhouse, where the ornate and traditional elements are balanced by the simple, almost austere way they are displayed. Soft shades of grey help to soften the look, while the white-painted floor makes it feel clean and contemporary.

*'Life is really simple, but we insist on making it complicated'*

Confucius

**THIS PAGE** A no-frills approach to decorating lends this 18th-century Swedish farmhouse a charming simplicity. Stripped floorboards, exposed rafters and minimal architectural detailing create the perfect backdrop for more decorative elements like the traditional ceramic stove and elegant Gustavian furniture.

Keeping it simple is not only a design decision; it is also a modern-day mantra that offers some welcome relief in our over-complicated, technology driven lives. Keeping it simple is about going back to basics, honing down our possessions, being kind to the planet, saving money, taking inspiration from humble things and working with what you have got. Many of us have been guilty at some time in our lives of thinking that the more we have – bigger house, up-to-date gadgets, better 'stuff' – the happier we will be, and it is easy to lose sight of what really matters. The *Pale & Interesting* take on simplicity is based on appreciating good, honest design, valuing quality not quantity and rediscovering simple pleasures.

The first step in embracing the simple life is to take a fresh look at your belongings. Ask yourself whether an object is useful. Do you love it? Has it got sentimental value? Does it improve your life in some way? Answering these questions will give you a good idea of what should stay and what should go. However, be cautious: the *Pale & Interesting* take on the simple home is not just about stripping your house back to the bare essentials. This is an altogether more human approach, so your aim is to edit your possessions while still retaining your sense of identity.

Storage is fundamental; an ordered, well-organized home will be tidy and clutter-free. Inevitably, we all have lots of paraphernalia that we don't want out on show – after all, there is only so far the editing process can go – but the way you house all your possessions needs careful consideration, especially when your ultimate aim is to

**ABOVE RIGHT** The polished concrete floor gives this simple Provençal gîte a contemporary feel. The grey dado painted around the lower part of the walls adds warmth and breaks up the space. Moroccan metal trays and a peeling oil painting lend just enough decorative interest to prevent the room from feeling stark.

**RIGHT** A painstaking attention to detail has been applied to the restoration of this Georgian scullery in the East End of London. Clean, plastered walls contrast beautifully with the rough rawness of the fireplace, which has been left in its original state. The subtle touches of colour soften the look and bring some warmth and homeliness.

create spaces that feel calm, spacious and pared down. One solution is to build in storage so that it appears to be part of the architecture of a room. Panelling a room straight across the chimney breast and alcoves, perhaps creating an integral fireplace as you go, offers an opportunity to build cupboards in the alcoves, while a bank of closets with touch-latch doors disguised as a wall of tongue-and-groove planking will fulfil the same function. Alternatively, make storage into a statement and choose freestanding pieces. Avoid mass-produced items and opt instead for well-crafted models in natural materials. They may cost more, but they will last a lifetime and you will be investing in the antiques of the future. If your budget won't stretch that far, or if you like the idea of buying into some history, then go for something old, such as an elegant antique French linen press, vintage blanket boxes or even wooden fruit crates that you can stack on their sides to create an unusual shelving system. Items like these have a timeless integrity, and buying antiques will not only add character to your interior but also helps to husband the planet's precious resources.

Even when decorating the simple way, every home needs some colour. As well as softening the look and banishing any coldness, colour can also be used to add contrast, accents and focal points. For instance, a couple of aqua linen cushions in an all-white scheme will offer a

**ABOVE** Despite the stone floor this elegant room has a sense of warmth, thanks to the white-washed timber-clad walls and the bergere chair upholstered in slubby linen. Stacked blanket boxes act as a console table while doubling up as storage. A faux vista has been created by transforming a salvaged window into a mirror, while the wooden trestle table adds utilitarian chic.

**RIGHT** An old railway clock sits happily alongside contemporary ceramics, a Le Klint lamp and a vintage camera to create an elegant yet very personal arrangement. Pulling together a disparate collection of items can be a challenging task, and one of the key ways to ensure that a display feels cohesive is to allow plenty of white space around it, as demonstrated here.

**THIS PAGE** Lots of white accents keeps this pretty dining room, painted in Farrow & Ball's Pink Ground, light and fresh. The bare floorboards and a workaday table and benches help ground the scheme, preventing it from feeling twee. A mismatched collection of vintage and antique plates is displayed on narrow shelves made from wooden batons to give the room a contemporary edge.

**THIS PAGE** A decorative wrought-iron lit bateau bed adds some feminine curves to this rather austere bedroom, while antique linen sheets, dyed a delicate dusky pink and sewn into a duvet cover and pillowcase, soften the grey and white scheme. The chandelier adds just a hint of glamour.

welcome place to rest your eye, while a strong neutral shade on one wall will bring depth and structure to a room. Just remember to keep colours soft and muted. Chalky pastels, off-whites, greys and neutrals will all add just the right amount of colour without being overbearing or fussy.

When it comes to furniture and accessories, less is definitely more. Stick to one or two key pieces and allow them plenty of space to breathe so that they can speak for themselves. Even highly decorative items or very disparate collections can look simple if they are displayed in the right way. An ornate antique gilt chair, for instance, will take on a clean and contemporary feel when placed in a sparsely decorated room, and a collection of mismatched and differently sized plates can be pulled into a coherent whole by displaying them en masse and keeping the rest of the interior very simple, so it does not compete.

**ABOVE** Modern metal-framed windows don't feel at all out of place in this old French gîte, serving merely to accentuate its rustic simplicity by contrasting with the uneven brick floor and the roughly plastered walls. A cosy armchair with a slipcover made from antique linen is the one concession to comfort.

**ABOVE RIGHT** Making the most of a small space, this tranquil bedroom in a city apartment takes on a grand feel thanks to the large panelled doors that lead onto it. Simple white-painted floorboards keep the whole look light and airy, and a couple of vintage cushions contribute a touch of colour.

**RIGHT** A clever use of basic materials brings textural interest to a guest bedroom in a cabin at the bottom of the garden. Reuse and recycle are at the heart of this room, where an old axle stand has found a new life as the base for a bedside table. The lamp is an original Anglepoise from a Lancaster bomber.

**THIS PAGE** Tongue-and-groove planking always creates a warm, relaxed feel and combined here with a reclaimed Bakelite railway station clock it takes on an easy vintage vibe. The chips and scuffs of the old enamel jug and the decommissioned metal dentist's drawers only add to the understated charm of this room. Freshly picked roses from the garden lend colour and femininity.

*keep it relaxed*

FORGET PRISTINE FURNITURE AND COORDINATING FABRICS. LET REAL LIFE BE YOUR DECORATING GUIDE BY CELEBRATING THE IMPERFECT AND EMBRACING FAMILY LIFE TO CREATE A LOOK THAT IS ALTOGETHER MORE LAID BACK.

**THIS PAGE** The open-plan arrangement of this Swedish apartment is perfectly suited to the busy but laid-back lifestyles of its musician and interior stylist owners and their young family. Easy- to-clean white-painted floorboards, plenty of art on the walls and a healthy mix of modern and vintage furniture and accessories create a home that is cosy and practical, yet effortlessly stylish.

BE CALM

**RIGHT** A casual approach to decorating lends this family dining room a comfortable and relaxed feel. The all-white colour scheme pulls together the mix-and-match collection of seemingly disparate elements. Although half of the room is packed with art, holiday souvenirs, books, magazines and other day-to-day items, the use of empty space elsewhere in the room, plus a flood of natural daylight from the balcony doors at one end, keeps it looking light, airy and clutter-free.

**OPPOSITE PAGE** A bold use of texture spells success in this laid-back living room in a converted factory in the South of France. Rough stone walls, exposed beams and limestone slabs have been cleverly layered with hand-woven linens, distressed paintwork, metal, paper and glass to create a scheme that is warm and welcoming and not at all precious, while the neutral palette of creams, whites, beiges and greys is calm and soothing.

A relaxed home is one that exudes a deep sense of comfort. We all have an instinctive desire to feel safe and cosseted in our own space, but that doesn't just mean surrounding yourself with squashy sofas, snug blankets and crisp cotton sheets. The key to creating a warm and welcoming interior is to pass on perfection and do away with design diktats. A laid-back, relaxed look stems from an easy-going attitude and clever use of contrast. Pair functional with decorative, elegant with casual, handmade with man-made and old with new. Let your home express your personality, and embrace the odd imperfection.

When it comes to decorating the relaxed way, anything that creates stress is out. That includes white carpets, any surface that requires a coaster before you can put a glass down, pale-coloured fitted upholstery that can't be removed and thrown in the washing machine and anything else that causes you to fret. Accept that inevitable spillages, scuffs and general wear and tear are part and parcel of daily life, and plan your interior accordingly. Depending on what kind of lifestyle you lead, make practical choices that will be party-proof, kid-proof, pet-proof…whatever is relevant to you.

Floors should be easy to clean, and stripped boards are practical, stylish and affordable. You may even have some lurking beneath your carpet waiting to be revealed, but if not, scour salvage yards for reclaimed boards. Opt for ecologically sound finishes such as eco-friendly paint, wax or Danish white soap. Flagstones and concrete are harder underfoot, but make up in practicality for what they lose in comfort, thus making you more relaxed on the maintenance front. If you yearn for a carpeted area, why not create a cosy snug in a small room where traffic is at a minimum; a special retreat for you and a chosen few.

The layout of your home can contribute to a more relaxed feel. Open-plan interiors lend themselves to a fluid, laid-back lifestyle, especially if you have young

children to keep an eye on. Families with teenagers, on the other hand, may want to close off areas to meet their growing need for privacy (not to mention your own!).

The dinner table should be at the heart of your home: a place to gather for family meals, large enough to accommodate dinner parties, homework, finger painting, pattern cutting or whatever else goes on in your home life. Try to pick the largest one you can comfortably fit into your space, preferably a sturdy piece full of character that you can scrub down after mealtimes and don't have to worry about.

Dining chairs don't all need to match: an eclectic mix of shapes and styles will only add to the atmosphere of your home.

When it comes to your sofa, it is worth spending as much as you can afford. As this is probably going to be one of your biggest investments, opt for something classic and timeless that won't go out of fashion and will stand the test of time. Make sure there are plenty of cushions to sink into and prop behind your head when you are snuggling down to read a book or watch television. If your budget will stretch to it, buy two sofas and place them

**ABOVE** The beauty of crumpled linen cushions is that the more you sit on the them, the better they look, like these ones made from antique sheets and grain sacks from Eastern Europe. Grouped together on a sunny window seat overlooking a beach, they offer the ideal spot for an afternoon nap.

**RIGHT** A cosy reading corner is home to a much-loved and well-worn armchair that has been carefully patched to face another day. Magazines are casually stacked on the floor, acting both as library and side table.

**OPPOSITE PAGE** In this deconstructed kitchen, a faded turquoise 1950s dresser and a slick stainless-steel cooker sit side by side, proving that old and new can complement each other perfectly. The splashback is an old piece of chequerboard enamelware from France.

'A home that does not have one worn comfy armchair in it is soulless'

May Sarton

**THIS PAGE** This 18th-century wrought-iron and marble table holds an array of family photographs of generations both past and present. Vintage mirrored photo frames add sparkle and a cake stand piled with shells and corals brings texture while keeping the arrangement personal.

**THIS PAGE** This relaxed and inviting bed is proof that elegance and a laid-back look can go hand in hand. Despite its minimalist style, piles of crisp cotton-covered pillows and a crumpled linen throw make this simple divan with no headboard feel like the height of luxury in this all-white bedroom. An old metal bin has been transformed into a quirky and unusual bedside table.

opposite each other to create a sociable sitting area, or hunt down a couple of deep leather armchairs to drag into a circle when numbers increase. A coffee table is essential and old trunks will do the job perfectly, as they also double up as extra storage. An abandoned metal factory stool or a wooden crate turned on its side works well as a side table.

Accessories and decorative details need the same light, easy touch as the rest of the house. There is no reason why kids' paintings shouldn't jostle alongside a treasured antique ornament inherited from your great aunt and an old clock you picked up at a car boot sale. The important thing is that everything you have out on display should have personal meaning for you and your family, and in that way your home will be a truly relaxed expression of yourselves.

# keep it real

DITCH FASHIONS AND TRENDS, CHOOSING INSTEAD TO
DECORATE YOUR HOME WITH DURABLE MATERIALS,
TIMELESS PIECES AND PERSONAL EXPRESSION TO CREATE
A HOME THAT HAS REAL HEART AND SOUL.

**OPPOSITE PAGE** This practical yet stylish kitchen has a pleasing rawness, due to the use of simple, natural materials and its unfussy style. Limewashed cupboard doors, cast-concrete shelving, reclaimed oak worksurfaces and glazed tiles all create texture and interest, while the pale colour scheme keeps it light and airy.

**THIS PAGE** No attempt has been made to conceal an extensive CD and vinyl collection in this Swedish apartment. Instead, it takes pride of place, becoming a focal point and an integral part of the room's décor. An Eames RAR rocker chair provides a comfy spot in which to sit and listen to the music.

I never read, I just look at pictures.

Andy Warhol

Moderna Museet, Stockholm Sweden 10/2-17/3 1968

**BELOW** Real life reigns in this eclectic kitchen, where the walls have been covered in photos of friends and family. A pistachio-green vintage-style fridge and light fitting provide a retro feel, while an old wooden bench has been stripped back to add some texture and warmth, offering a cosy nook to relax in.

**OPPOSITE PAGE** For a pretty yet practical effect, newspaper has been cut in a zigzag pattern and used to create a decorative edging for these kitchen shelves. They are home to a well-loved collection of Cornish Blue pottery and pastel-coloured vintage china in soft shades of pale green, powder blue and cream.

A real home is one that reflects the lifestyles and personalities of its occupants. With the media constantly telling us what to wear, what to do and how to do it, it can be hard to keep a perspective on what really matters in life.

The *Pale & Interesting* ethos demands that you be true to yourself. Forget fleeting fashions and passing trends, and instead focus on creating an interior that works for all its inhabitants, both practically and visually. Give your home plenty of soul by adorning your space with the things that you love. It doesn't matter that your cherished 1960s tulip table doesn't exactly match your grandmother's Chippendale chair, or if your husband's record collection takes over half the sitting room. Instead, allow these familiar items to take pride of place; that way, they will tell the story of your life and from that your very own style will naturally evolve.

In the *Pale & Interesting* home, the notion of keeping it real also extends to using natural materials and finishes. Choose objects that will improve with age rather than throwaway alternatives that may initially seem like a cheap option but won't stand the test of time. This is a look where furniture is valued for signs of wear and tear, handcrafted objects are cherished for their individuality and utilitarian items are celebrated for their functionality.

Natural materials are a good place to start when thinking about the structure of your home. Wood, plaster, brick and stone all have an honest simplicity that will not only send the right visual messages and add texture and soul to your home but will also prove to be durable and practical. Bare plaster, for instance, has a beautiful soft bloom to it that actually improves with age. If you don't like the sludgy pink colour, hunt out a plasterer who is happy to work with the white version, which is the elegant shade of alabaster.

**THIS PAGE** A clever mix of styles gives this designer's living room a relaxed and truly individual flavour. Furniture has been left in a 'found' state, embracing the scuffs and chips that tell stories of previous lives, while vintage florals sit happily alongside a faded antique kelim. A collection of American tin ceiling tiles are hung on the wall to create a panelled effect.

**RIGHT** The owners of this elegant Huguenot house have taken a purist approach to its renovation, stripping the interior back to its original state and only using reclaimed materials to retain the building's integrity. The soft heritage colours used throughout the house keep a feeling of authenticity, and the antique country furniture brings a simple, understated charm.

**ABOVE** The structural bones of this wooden cabin have been laid bare to add depth and texture to the all-white scheme. Two well-worn 1920s leather armchairs sit comfortably on the wooden floor, confidently displaying their obvious signs of wear and tear, which gives them character and the interior a relaxed appeal. A wood-burning stove ensures that the space is always warm and cosy, even on cold days.

On the walls, wooden planking will add a dash of down-to-earth rustic charm. Make sure that you use recycled or sustainably sourced wood, if possible. Alternatively, you might consider exposing the rafters in the ceiling for a pared-back, functional look. In fact, stripping back what is already there, scraping off layers of paint or pulling off plasterboard to reveal the house's structure beneath, is a great way to 'decorate', as it allows you to appreciate the bare bones of your home. You will be amazed at what you uncover. Beautiful paint colours chosen by previous owners in different eras, small fragments of

wallpaper, thick beams, original tiles that have been partly concreted over; all these remnants have a rawness that will add depth and interest.

Finishes should be simple and understated. Reclaimed floorboards, for instance, could be left bare, unsanded and unfinished, allowing their patina to continue to develop, just as you would with York stone. If you are laying new boards, don't even think about varnishing them. Instead, bleach them with lye for a cool Scandinavian feel, or paint them with eco-friendly floor paint. Either way, allow them to develop their own signs of wear and tear over time.

Furniture should be useful. There is something gratifying and aesthetically pleasing about a piece that does its job properly. The Shakers maintained that there is 'beauty in utility', and this approach is just what is needed in the *Pale & Interesting* home. Whenever possible, choose vintage or antique pieces over newly made items – after all, why chop down another tree to make a table when a perfectly good one already exists? Don't immediately discard something that is a little tired and worn: flaking paint, rusty legs or battered leather all tell the story of a past life and confirm an item's authenticity. If you are going for something new, opt for handcrafted pieces that will age gracefully and, in time, will be able to tell their own stories.

Natural fabrics are the right choice for a *Pale & Interesting* interior – good-quality linen, cotton, denim and wool are all ideal candidates. A sofa upholstered in a thick, heavyweight canvas will age and wear over time in much the same way as a wooden table, developing worn patches and faded areas that will only add to its modest charm. In the same way, linen sheets and woollen blankets will gently soften and improve with age, as long as they are cared for properly.

**ABOVE** This antique radiator, with its original green peeling paint intact, was salvaged from a local reclamation yard to become a stunning focal point in this whitewashed beach house. A vintage Welsh blanket picks up on the minty green hue.

**LEFT** Raw materials are left to speak for themselves in this charming rustic cabin. A selection of mismatched reclaimed planks has been used to clad the walls and the resulting slightly uneven effect brings interest and depth. The recycled scaffolding boards on the floor have been left as they were found, unsanded and untreated, to make the most of their patina.

**OPPOSITE PAGE** The owners of this Victorian townhouse have made a feature of the brick chimney stacks by leaving them exposed in this light and airy attic room. The all-white scheme pulls together an eclectic assortment of items on the antique metal table, while the original 1970s Harry Bertoia Diamond chair adds a retro twist.

'The strength of a nation derives from the integrity of the home'

Confucius

THE KEY TO A SUCCESSFUL *PALE & INTERESTING* INTERIOR IS TO GENTLY INTRODUCE SOFT COLOUR IN SUBTLE WAYS TO CREATE ROOM SCHEMES THAT FEEL LIGHT AND AIRY BUT NEVER ANAEMIC OR WASHED OUT.

**THIS PAGE** A pale grey cupboard adds a hint of colour to a monochrome scheme. A classic BTC Hector lamp combines with handcrafted and antique ceramics in various neutral shades to create a calm and contemporary still life. The black-and-white photograph is by Jake Curtis.

*shades of pale*

**THIS PAGE** This beautifully restored 18th-century Huguenot house has been painted an elegant shade of duck-egg blue. Accents of white add focus, while the animal skin and retro glass bowl help to mix things up and make sure that the room doesn't feel like a Georgian pastiche.

Colour is an essential part of any home. It adds depth, creates focal points, can seemingly alter the proportions or style of a room, provides an outlet for personal expression and, above all, demands an emotional response. The way in which colour influences our moods is a very personal thing and can strongly affect the feel of your home, so choosing the right palette can be a daunting task.

In the *Pale & Interesting* home, the aim is to create schemes that have a pale, tranquil feel without feeling cold or unwelcoming. Think of soft and unobtrusive colours that gently calm the senses and you will be on the right track. Chalky pastels, earthy neutrals, off-whites, shades of grey, vintage-style ice-cream hues or elegant taupes are all perfect for a light and airy interior.

Inspiration can come from many sources: magazine tear sheets, scraps of fabric, a walk on the beach, a vintage table in a delicious shade of pistachio green that you picked up at a fleamarket or even just a flower from the garden. Any of these could kickstart a stream of ideas for your scheme. Similarly, there are many different ways of introducing colour: walls, fabrics, furniture and accessories are all good means by which you can showcase your chosen palette. The next step is to decide what kind of scheme you are going for. You may like the idea of painting the whole house in subtle pastels to achieve a soft harmonious feel, or perhaps you are hoping to create

**ABOVE** A mix of rustic simplicity and industrial chic keeps the kitchen of this beach house looking fresh and new. A powder-blue range-style cooker provides a strong shot of colour, which is echoed in the vintage enamelware and ceramics. Glossy subway-style tiles help to reflect light back into the room, while oversized reproduction factory lights play with scale.

**RIGHT** Reclaimed glazed doors have been cleverly reused in combination with simple planking to create a contemporary dresser with a rustic feel. The tasteful collection of antique English creamware and Swedish 18th- and 19th-century porcelain are offset beautifully by the delicate pink interior of the cabinet, which accentuates the elegant and graceful shapes of the china.

**THIS PAGE** The success of this room lies in the combination of masculine and feminine elements, which come together to create a balanced look. Pretty pastel colours bring the bleached-out interior to life. The chipped paint on the ice-cream pink table prevents it from looking too girly, and the pale blue cushion cover is made from French antique mattress ticking. A chunky task light and simple aluminium hanging shade add a utilitarian feel, as does the battered enamel sign on the wall.

contrast with pops of colour in an all-white scheme. Alternatively, you might lean towards a more tonal look, taking inspiration from nature by layering earthy browns and beiges.

Colour on the walls is a strong statement, so choose soft, subtle tones that won't jump out at you. Vibrant brights are best left to accessories in the *Pale & Interesting* home. Natural paints with a high chalk content are particularly suitable, as they are kinder to the environment and their matt finish also complements these sorts of colours in just the right way, bringing texture and depth to plain plastered walls. Another way to add interest

**THIS PAGE** A delicate palette of grey and white lends the rustic interior of this 18th-century Swedish farmhouse an air of calm elegance. The mixture of modern chain-store furniture and antiques banishes any suggestion of a laboured homage to days gone by, despite the meticulous restoration of the original panelled walls, making the room up to date and relevant to modern family living.

to large expanses of wall is to take inspiration from the art of trompe l'oeil and paint large panels of coordinating colours on the walls. Not only will this break up the walls in larger rooms but it can also exaggerate or improve a room's proportions to make ceilings appear higher or, conversely, help to make a cavernous space feel cosier. Be bold with battleship-grey panels on a paler pebble-grey background, or go for a more subtle approach with milky shades of off-white. Wallpaper can be another great way to introduce some colour, although you will need to keep the other elements in the room pared down to maintain that all-important atmosphere of calm serenity.

THIS PAGE In this opulent yet low-key dwelling, an elegant 19th-century French daybed sits against simple painted walls. Rectangles of Farrow & Ball's Hardwick White have been painted onto a background of Shaded White to offer a contemporary take on traditional panelling. The pared-back arrangement tones down the highly decorative elements of a silk damask-covered chaise and crystal wall sconces, while the addition of a 1950s occasional table adds a retro twist. The muted pastel palette keeps the overall feel warm and welcoming.

*Think of soft and unobtrusive colours that gently calm the senses*

An all-white scheme will need to have some colour somewhere, whether it is in the shape of curtains, cushions, furniture or simply a vaseful of acid-green foliage picked from the garden. Antique French and Swedish furniture comes in beautiful soft shades and is perfect if you are looking to create a sense of shabby elegance. However, if antiques are beyond your budget, take inspiration from their delicate, faded hues and paint junk-shop finds in the same gentle greys and blues for a thrifty alternative. Other options include painting every chair around the dining table a different colour for an eclectic effect, displaying a collection of coloured jugs on open shelves or hanging curtains in a bold vintage floral for a splash of retro chic.

Soft furnishings offer an ideal opportunity to introduce your chosen shades. Loose slipcovers in gorgeous pastel hues of lilac, lemon yellow or dusky pink will add just a hint of femininity, but if you are leaning towards a more masculine look, opt for something stronger, such as slate grey or denim, making sure you incorporate accents of lighter colours in the form of cushions and throws.

Colour can also be introduced in the shape of more practical items, such as kitchen equipment, storage units, books, table linen or even your everyday china. Paying attention to these small details will help enrich your scheme and ensure you enjoy it on a day-to-day basis.

**FAR LEFT** A 1950s faux marble-topped occasional table in a beautiful shade of soft green provides the perfect backdrop for delicate apricot-coloured garden roses in a contemporary handcrafted cream bowl.

**LEFT** Vintage Welsh blankets come in an amazing array of retro pastels, soft neutrals and stronger shades, and are perfect for adding a dash of colour to an all-white scheme.

**ABOVE** An ageing 1930s eiderdown, lovingly patched to see another day, softens up a classic 18th-century Gustavian daybed. Bare, white-soaped boards and plain planked walls keep the background clean and simple, providing a blank canvas for the eclectic combination of muted English florals and an ethnic print at the window, both of which introduce colour to the interior in a subtle but interesting way.

**THIS PAGE** Shades of grey. This serene living room uses a spectrum of greys ranging from pebble and battleship through to charcoal and slate to create a modern classic look. A large mirror propped casually between the two windows helps to reflect light back into this already bright space while also providing an attractive view of the opposite side of the room.

**ABOVE** A simple band of grey paint creates a dado effect and gives a bold yet understated injection of colour to this rustic room. A contemporary bed base is draped in antique French linen sheets and an old factory stool makes a bedside table. A row of plates on the wall is the only concession to ornamentation.

**ABOVE RIGHT** A country bench painted a zingy apple green adds a vibrant touch of colour to this otherwise stark hallway.

**RIGHT** A contemporary take on a traditional toile de Jouy: this wallpaper by Manuel Canovas has been coloured an exquisite shade of powder blue and is used to maximum effect in this pretty feminine bedroom. An old and rather worn cupboard adds an element of shabby chic, while a set of distressed metal shutters stands in as a fire-screen. Old fruit crates offer some extra storage on top of the wardrobe, and the 1960s plastic light shade contributes a hint of retro cool.

**THIS PAGE AND OPPOSITE** A perfect lesson in the use of texture in an all-white interior. A huge, luxurious armchair is covered in slubby linen and softened with a sumptuous mohair blanket. A pair of old louvre shutters, boasting their original peeling paint, add depth and interest to the white walls. On the mantelpiece, a rich and interesting display of objects, including an old bottle, dried hydrangeas, pieces of coral, a sea anemone, a pile of antique books and an old enamel numberplate, creates a focal point in gentle neutral shades.

ENSURE THAT YOUR HOME HAS DEPTH AND INTEREST BY EXPLORING THE USE OF TEXTURE AND FORM. TAKE INSPIRATION FROM NATURE AND COMBINE ROUGH WITH SMOOTH, GEOMETRIC WITH ORGANIC AND LIGHT WITH DARK.

*texture and form*

Texture and form are key to creating a successful interior. Without these two essential factors, you will end up with a cold, bland scheme that is lacking in depth and interest. Light colours can sometimes all merge into one, and it is the texture and form contributed by walls, floors, fabrics, furniture and objects that add a sense of perspective, dimension and definition to an interior.

Once you start exploring the use of these two magic components, you will discover that nature is always your best teacher. Think of glistening water lapping at soft sand, powdery snow dusting rough bark or ripe round pears dangling from twisted branches. Everywhere you look there is a lesson in texture and form from which you can glean ideas.

Texture is the characteristic of an object or surface in terms of the way it looks and feels. In general, smooth, shiny or silky surfaces, such as mirror, lacquer or satin, are considered to create a formal environment, while heavier, coarser ones, like weathered wood, stone or linen, lend themselves to a more relaxed look. While you don't need to follow hard-and-fast rules when it comes to decorating, it is a good idea to get to grips with these concepts before you start playing around with them. Think of texture as a paint palette and combine surfaces as you would colours, sometimes blending them, sometimes contrasting them, and in this way you will be able to build up layers of texture and a sense of depth, shaping your interior to suit you.

Roughly hewn wood planking, bare brick or, for a more elegant take on the theme, Georgian-style panelling are all ideal ways in which to introduce texture to walls. Scour reclaimation yards for salvaged panelling, rafters or shutters that you may be able to adapt into wall coverings. Treat what's underfoot in the same way. Old scaffolding boards make brilliant floorboards. Leave them as they are – plaster dust, paint splashes and all – or sand them back, bleach and limewash them. Concrete and stone are great in warmer climates or with underfloor heating, and can also be combined with wood to create a kind of panelled effect on the floor.

Furniture offers ample possibilities when it comes to texture. Rusty metal tables, old armoires with peeling

**OPPOSITE PAGE** Texture and form are important tools in the *Pale & Interesting* interior and can be used in many ways. Pebbles, decorative ceramics, corals, tactile fabrics or old books will all add definition and sensuality to your home.

**LEFT** This decorative stone and plasterwork fireplace adds both texture and form to a simple interior. The refinement of the porcelain figurine and decorative glass offers an effective contrast to the raw textures of the room.

**ABOVE** Contrast and blend textures to play up their differences and similarities. Here, a glass cake stand has been piled with corals and shells in a variety of shapes and textures to create a centrepiece on a marble-topped table. The carved marble hands add matt smoothness, while the mirror has a rich patina that is almost ghostly.

**THIS PAGE** The beautiful stone walls of what was once a factory in Provence are allowed to speak for themselves in this sparse interior, which has been furnished in a simple and functional way. Metal stacking chairs are juxtaposed with a country-style wooden table, a raw linen tablecloth softens any hard lines and the mercury glass candlesticks add twinkle and glamour.

**ABOVE** Simple textures combine to decorative effect in this contemporary living room. A heap of logs has been piled in the minimalist fireplace as a way to deal with the 'black hole' problem during the summer months, and a stack of felted floor cushions and cosy blankets sits in front, offering extra seating should unexpected guests arrive.

**ABOVE LEFT** This contemporary kitchen uses contrasting textures to great effect. Cast-concrete units sit beside a stainless-steel range-style cooker. Recycled wood crates slide onto shelves for a deconstructed look, and a skylight floods the area with light. Sleek custom-built cabinets provide plenty of storage to ensure a streamlined feel.

paint, squashy sofas covered in slubby linens or shiny mirror-topped tables will all blend and contrast perfectly. But it is the soft furnishings and accessories that really allow you to complete the picture. Hand-thrown ceramic bowls filled with shells, piles of tactile blankets and throws, crisp cotton pillows and twinkling glass all act as focal points to create that pivotal sense of definition, but also to feed our senses.

It is form that gives a room structure, perspective and visual appeal. Form affects the look, mood and style of an interior and comes into play when choosing furniture, accessories and architectural details. Straight edges will provide an ordered framework, while curved edges add femininity, softening the atmosphere and appearance of the scheme. By juxtaposing complementary or contrasting forms – for example a collection of objects along a mantelpiece or a mismatched selection of chairs in a living room – you are, in a sense, composing a landscape with a foreground and background that will add depth and interest in much the same way as texture does. Contrasting form is also important for keeping the balance right. For instance, if you have a square, chunky sofa, then you will want to lighten the look by adding some spindly, leggy pieces, such as a delicate French metal café table, or something more curvaceous and organic, like a classic Eames lounge chair.

Light and dark also define form and play a key role in creating focal points or to help ground an all-white room. A pair of white linen curtains will be given form by the shadows in the folds that help them to hold their shape, and you can mimic this effect in other areas of your room using varying shades of whites, off-whites and greys, accenting them with small blocks of contrasting colours to give the scheme some weight.

**THIS PAGE** Simple integral shelving supports have been built into the thickness of the wall to create a simple dresser effect.

**ABOVE** Elegant plaster casts of an antique gilt flower carving and a pair of old pattern-cutting scissors sit beside two glass bottles, bringing balance and contrast to this mantelpiece arrangement. The deep pink peonies add a shot of unexpected colour.

**OPPOSITE PAGE** The owners of this chic living room have achieved a great sense of perspective and depth, due to clever use of form. They have layered substantial, solid pieces of furniture, like the handsome sofa and the elegant bergere, with more leggy 'see-through' pieces, such as the metal chaise and the wooden trestle table. The vista all the way through to the kitchen in the background further extends the sense of space.

**THIS PAGE** This interior showcases a number of seemingly discordant elements by giving each piece space to breathe. The boxy 1970s leather swivel chair offers a relaxing retreat in which to read a book beneath the sensual curves of the Le Klint light, while a pile of cushions on the floor softens the harshness of the room's minimalist treatment.

**THIS PAGE** An ultra-feminine Victorian button-back slipper chair is brought into the 21st century when combined with a simple, contemporary paper lamp and a slick modern mirror. Frosted glass at the window ensures privacy in this spartan bedroom, where curtains would be too fussy.

# mixing it up

EXPLORE THE ART OF CONTRAST AND HAVE FUN DECORATING YOUR SPACE WITH A BOLD MIX OF STYLES AND GENRES TO CREATE A HOME THAT IS ENTIRELY PERSONAL AND UNIQUE.

The *Pale & Interesting* philosophy is all about mixing it up. Forget clichéd themes or trends; this look is all about individuality and the art of contrast. What you are aiming for is a healthy mix of styles to keep the look current and relevant to your lifestyle. Combining retro with classical, antique with modern, oriental with European or femininity with utility will add interest, bring a dash of humour and keep the overall effect lively and personal. The crucial thing is to maintain a pared-down background, so that an interior never looks cluttered or over-complicated. Trust in your own taste and you will create a home that reflects your personality and showcases the things you love.

Quite often, an interior that mixes several different styles and looks is one that has evolved organically over time; where family heirlooms, quirky finds and practical purchases coexist happily alongside each other. You can recreate an interior with the same sort of feel. Whether you are going for a full-on eclectic vibe or simply want to enliven an otherwise coordinated scheme with a few deliberate clashes, you will need somewhere to begin and the architecture of a room offers plenty of opportunities for contrasting and mixing.

Start by identifying the room's strongest characteristic, be it modern, traditional, distressed or formal, and then set out to

**ABOVE AND RIGHT** This old French country house has been given a modern makeover yet still retains its rustic charm. The traditional, utilitarian cast-concrete units have been fitted with modern drawers, and a slick contemporary tap/faucet is given iconic status in its own little hand-plastered alcove. Rough-hewn slabs of slate act as a minimalist splashback and the moulded polypropylene chairs contrast beautifully with the old scrubbed wood farmhouse table.

*Trust in your own taste and you will create a home that reflects your personality.*

**THIS PAGE** A beautifully proportioned refectory table with unusual tapered legs is offset by a set of vintage injection-moulded mass-produced chairs, just as the roughly plastered walls act as a foil to the polished concrete floor. The grey paint below dado height offers a practical solution to the inevitable scrapes and scuffs that appear on white walls while also acting to cleverly frame the composition.

**THIS PAGE** A clever mix of elements here, where original Lincrusta wall covering, painted white, offers a decorative backdrop to an elegant 1960s sideboard boasting an impressive collection of post-war coloured glass. A clean-lined contemporary sofa has been covered in a vibrant acid-yellow chintzy fabric to create a room scheme that is a true amalgamation of styles and genres.

deliberately find a foil for that element. For instance, a sleek Cappellini sofa would look stunning in the formal grandeur of a Georgian panelled room, whereas an elegant antique gilt mirror would create the same effect in a slick, architect-designed, minimalist cube, and an elegant French country dining table could soften an industrial warehouse space. Similarly, you can play with flooring by placing a chunky, roughly textured coffee table made from reclaimed railway sleepers on a smooth, white-painted concrete floor, or a delicate, antique console table on battered, untreated wooden boards. Kitchens and bathrooms also offer a chance to inject contrast into the home. Think of concrete shelves stacked with wicker drawers, stainless-steel units with honed marble worksurfaces or copper piping with a shiny, contemporary ceramic sink.

The furniture you choose has a part to play. A set of vintage French metal files, stacked to create a side table, will bring utility chic to an elegant bergere chair, while a Moroccan pouffe could add an ethnic twist to a traditional Chesterfield sofa. The way you finish or dress a piece of furniture will also have an influence on the final scheme. Try covering a modern piece, like a boxy Antonio Citterio daybed, in a pretty vintage floral to add femininity to an otherwise masculine design, or strip off the upholstery on a carved, Louis-style bedhead to reveal the wooden frame, and paint it a cool graphite for a dash of pared-back chic.

Lighting is another way to take the look in a different direction. Hang a retro pendant beside elegant 18th-century antiques or an industrial-style lamp alongside pretty florals. Many lighting companies are already fusing styles within their designs, playing with traditional and modern idioms to produce new takes on old themes – think of Habitat's Spindle light, which is a modern version of the dated standard lamp, or Moooi's paper chandelier.

Accessories are your chance to be bold. Try throwing richly embellished saris over beaten-up leather armchairs, arranging fossils alongside fluid 1960s glassware, hanging lustrous mirrors beside antique antlers, suspending Chinese lanterns next to English chintz or placing hand-thrown pottery next to vintage candlesticks.

**ABOVE RIGHT** Victorian grandeur is tempered by feminine contemporary touches in this elegant through sitting room. Lofty ceilings, pale grey walls and white-painted woodwork and floorboards provide a clean, unfussy backdrop for an adventurous combination of styles, which ensures that this interior feels fresh, lively and personal.

**BOTTOM RIGHT** The highly patterned encaustic tiled floor is the centrepiece of this simple family kitchen, where painted chairs combine with the clean lines of a retro 1950s table. Modern units are topped with wooden worksurfaces and splashbacks salvaged from the science lab in an old school that still proudly bear the graffiti of past pupils.

**THIS PAGE** Nearly everything in this charming rustic cabin has been reclaimed or recycled, from the mismatched timber plank walls, old French school posters and bed linen made from antique linen sheets that have been dyed grey, to the bedside table made from an old axle stand and off-cut of scaffolding along with the original anglepoise taken from a wartime aircraft.

**OPPOSITE PAGE** The key to recycling is to think outside the box. Here, an old wooden crate has been transformed into a practical side table. A reconditioned vintage phone contrasts nicely with the modern Hector lamp, while a metal tub filled with architectural leaves adds some colour to this otherwise neutral scheme.

CELEBRATE THE BEAUTY OF THE IMPERFECT AND EMBRACE THE ART OF REUSE, REPAIR AND RECYCLING FOR A RESPONSIBLE APPROACH TO DECORATING THAT WON'T INCREASE YOUR CARBON FOOTPRINT OR BREAK THE BANK.

While we all try and do our bit by carrying bottles to the bottle bank, recyling newspapers and taking our own bags to the supermarket, we still live in a throwaway society in which mass-produced, disposable items are being manufactured at a frightening rate. Recycling and reusing are essential to the *Pale & Interesting* ethos. Not only do they they lighten the load on the world's natural resources but they are also easy on your pocket and will help you to create an individual one-off style that cannot be bought on the high street.

*waste not want not*

**THIS PAGE** Furniture and accessories that show signs of wear and tear are like dear old friends, full of warmth and character. Here in this whitewashed beach hut, a battered metal trunk does double duty as a coffee table and extra storage. Combined with the well-loved leather armchair, the look here is warm, welcoming and not at all precious.

**OPPOSITE ABOVE LEFT** Mixing various components, such as this vintage metal jelly mould, woven flex and incandescent squirrel cage lightbulb (based on an original 1930s model), make this light fitting a stunning focal point.

**OPPOSITE ABOVE CENTRE** Antique grain sacks seems to be eternally useful. This one has been used to create a Swedish-style roller blind.

**OPPOSITE ABOVE RIGHT** An old Kilner jar has been given a new lease of life as a light fitting. The top is drilled with holes to keep it well ventilated.

**BELOW** An old linen sheet that was beyond repair has been cut up and turned into cushions. The original monogram has been retained and used to patch a small hole, creating a unique decorative detail.

**BELOW CENTRE** A shelf liner made from old newspaper shows that there is beauty in all things, if only you care to see it.

**BELOW RIGHT** A much-loved armchair has been repaired with a piece of vintage Sanderson floral linen union. Opting for a boldly contrasting fabric instead of trying to conceal the patch makes a charming feature.

The notion of 'waste not want not' is also about investing in good-quality products that are made to last and then looking after them carefully. For example, linen sheets represent a huge investment and should last a lifetime. If they develop a hole, darn it, and once they lose their whiteness, dye them and allow the colour to fade gracefully over time. We should all be brushing up on the skills of darning, patching and mending. It makes good ecological and economical sense, and it also affords the opportunity to put your own stamp on the antiques of the future. These painstaking repairs only add to an item's intrinsic charm. The key is to buy classic styles that won't date.

**BELOW** This antique carved marble sink supported on cast-concrete legs has a timeless feel. The tap was fashioned from a length of copper piping, while the decorative lead splashback adds a practical yet decorative element. Crystal sconces bring some glamour and sparkle to this minimalist bathroom.

**RIGHT** These 1970s teak-backed aluminium hooks were salvaged from a school that was being refurbished. They have now found a new home in a bedroom, providing a home for a display of necklaces and bangles.

**FAR RIGHT** Don't discard an item just because it is a little battered and bruised. Such scars bring interest and history to your home. Pieces like this torn 1920s French leather club chair are becoming hard to find these days, and even with the damage they are quite collectable.

Salvaging items requires imagination and dogged perseverance. Haunt salvage yards, yard sales, jumble sales and thrift stores, visiting them as often as you can – you never know when the perfect find will turn up. Be creative when hunting for old furniture. One man's junk is another man's treasure. Don't think that you have to invest in fine antiques, or use objects for what they were originally intended. Look beyond the obvious, and see things with a fresh eye. Old tea towels can be transformed into cushion covers, faded sailcloths fashioned into curtains, office furniture turned into bedroom storage, tin ceiling tiles used as bathroom splashback and old hooks converted into toilet roll holders – these are all perfect examples of items that have been adapted for a new use.

Architectural reclamation companies are a recycler's dream. They are overflowing with everything from building materials like old doors, bricks and radiators to more elaborate items such as roll-top bathtubs, panelling and furniture. Once you have got your home kitted out with the basics, you can then think about drawing on these amazing resources to create unusual features. Why not fit an old window with mirrored glass to make a stunning centrepiece to your hallway? Old shutters can be transformed into fitted cupboards – don't worry if they don't all match, as it will only add character – or a pile of roof slates can be given a new lease of life as a tabletop.

Don't dismiss the hardware department either: old doorknobs make fantastic coat hooks, while cast-iron sink brackets can support kitchen shelves.

Second-hand furniture will bear testament to its previous lives. Scuffs, scratches and general wear and tear should be seen as positive attributes; a patina that gives articles authenticity and individuality. However, the finish on some pieces may be too far gone, or perhaps you like an item's shape but not its colour. In these cases, give them a new lease of life with a coat of paint. The same applies to fabrics. A tattered old Welsh blanket or quilted bedspread could be cut up to make cushion covers, and antique linen sheets that are threadbare in the middle can be transformed into pillowcases. If you have a pile of vintage fabric remnants, don't discard them. Use them for wrapping presents or creating cards, or you could even embark on making a patchwork quilt. After all, crafting activities have lost their fuddy-duddy associations in the last few years and are now firmly back in vogue.

**THIS PAGE** This industrial powder-coated metal fold-up stand has found a new life as a coffee table and offers the perfect resting place for these freshly picked hydrangeas displayed in an old milk jug. In the background an antique grain sack has been fashioned into a cushion cover, while the floorboards are reclaimed scaffolding planks.

# collecting

**THIS PAGE** Old books and
vintage mixing bowls are
displayed on high shelves in this
light and airy hallway. The shelf
attached to the ceiling has been
ingeniously designed to disguise
an unsightly steel girder. A
collection of old railway carriage
numbers has been put to use as
a decorative feature on the
bedroom doors.

BECOME YOUR OWN CURATOR AND DISCOVER NEW AND INTERESTING WAYS TO DISPLAY YOUR TREASURED POSSESSIONS SO THAT THEY DON'T FEEL LIKE CLUTTER.

**THIS PAGE** A beautiful wooden model sailing boat gives this pale bedroom a nautical theme. Placing it beside a couple of fossils and piles of antique books shows that a creative mix-and-match approach to displaying your collections will ensure that your home never looks like a museum.

*Soothing colours and tactile fabrics will help turn your space into a relaxing retreat where you can put your feet up and unwind.*

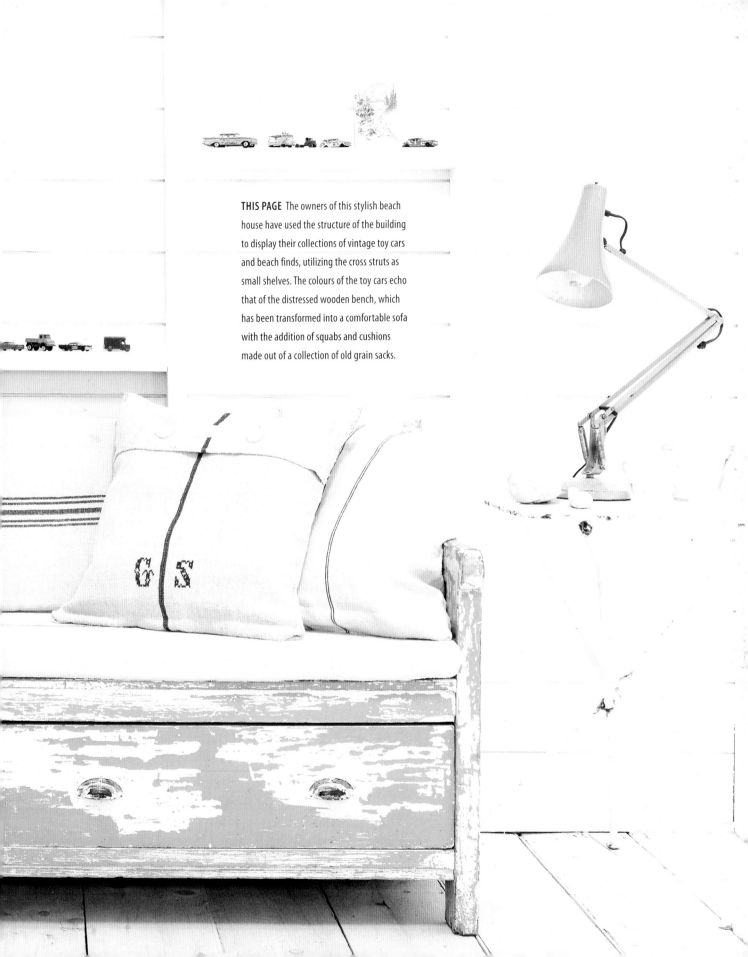

**THIS PAGE** The owners of this stylish beach house have used the structure of the building to display their collections of vintage toy cars and beach finds, utilizing the cross struts as small shelves. The colours of the toy cars echo that of the distressed wooden bench, which has been transformed into a comfortable sofa with the addition of squabs and cushions made out of a collection of old grain sacks.

The simple life is all very well, but collecting is a human instinct and few of us would want to live without our cherished possessions around us. The trick is to know how to display your treasures in a way that allows them to be appreciated without taking over your space. Be your own curator and train yourself to have a discerning eye, only giving your favourite and most worthy items floor and shelf space. In this way, you will create focal points in your home that are striking and personal.

Almost anything is collectable. The *Compact Oxford English Dictionary* defines a collection as 'A group of accumulated items of a particular kind', so whatever your obsession, it deserves to be displayed, as long as the components relate in some way to each other or are unified either by their nature or the way in which they are presented.

Old tins, hats, shells that have been gathered on various family holidays, toys, bits of driftwood, paintings, bottles or even vintage tools would all make pleasing displays.

The first step in successful curating is to declutter your home. Good storage is indispensable. Try to create a place for everything and keep everything in its place and you will be halfway there. Think about which items you want to keep tucked away out of sight and which you want out on show, as some of your storage will actually become part of the room's decoration, especially if it is showing off your collection of vintage magazines or 19th-century lustreware. Some units have both solid and glazed doors so that they can do double duty in both concealing and exhibiting, and this is particularly useful in smaller homes.

You will need to exercise a degree of self-control when it comes to displaying your precious exhibits. For an effective display, you don't need to have absolutely everything out at the same time – ringing the changes keeps things interesting. You may have dozens of beautiful ceramic jugs, but if you rotate the items out on display and only show a select few at a time, you will keep the collection looking fresh. Another idea is to change your displays

**OPPOSITE PAGE** Be your own curator and ensure that only the best pieces are allowed shelf space. You don't need to display every single item in your collection at any one time. Rotate the pieces on display and that way you will appreciate them all the more. This pretty selection of lustreware is given room to breathe, which keeps the overall effect fresh and uncluttered. The decorative painted-glass panel on the 19th-century clock echoes the pretty pastel pink of the china.

**ABOVE** An interesting grouping of off-white ceramic pots and jugs, enamel labels and house numbers reveals this homeowner's passion for old typefaces. The pale blue interior of the cupboard helps the collection to stand out.

**RIGHT** An attractive assemblage of rare Victorian engraved mirrors brightens up a dull corner. An early 19th-century tin clock sits comfortably in the centre.

**ABOVE** An eclectic and very personal compilation of vintage signs, decorative objects and local artists' work have been hung closely together on a wall to create a striking display on the landing of this family home in South East England.

**RIGHT** This imposing open-fronted cabinet holds an array of china and glass, proving that everyday objects can form an aesthetically pleasing decorative display. A grey linen-covered beanbag on the high-gloss white floor offers a comfy spot to relax.

on a seasonal basis, perhaps with shells and beachcombing finds showcased during the summer months, for example, and autumn leaves, seedpods and twigs in the winter.

The manner in which you display your collections will also have a bearing on the overall effect. Random arrangements have a habit of merging into everyday clutter, so a sense of order is essential. Hanging pieces on the wall in regimented lines and rows, arranging them symmetrically on shelves or grouping items together by theme will all create a connection that draws many disparate pieces into a unified whole.

If you prefer a less regulated and more relaxed look, make sure there is plenty of empty space around your collection and this will also tie different objects together into a coherent whole.

For example, an eclectic mix of different-sized paintings, photos and posters in mismatched frames can be pulled together if they are hung en masse, keeping the gaps between them small. The rest of the room should also be kept simple.

Another way to connect your collections is to display them under glass to create a museum-like atmosphere. Glazed cabinets, old retail units, glass cloches, cake covers, jam pots or apothecary jars are all perfect for the job. The plan is to be in control of your collection and not the other way around.

Collections can also be used to alter the proportions of the room. A single row of plates, for instance, hung at eye level could help the ceiling seem higher while a wall packed with antlers would make a large space feel more intimate.

**THIS PAGE** An impressive collection of antlers, butterflies, fossils and shells massed together creates maximum impact in this interior. An eclectic yet stylish mix of furniture and accessories keeps the look up to date, while vintage floral cushions add a touch of femininity. Clean white walls ensure that the overall feel is fresh.

IN ORDER TO MEET EVERYONE'S NEEDS, A SUCCESSFUL LIVING ROOM MUST BE
ADAPTABLE AND PRACTICAL; BOTH A RELAXING RETREAT AND A FUNCTIONAL,
MULTI-TASKING FAMILY ROOM.

**THIS PAGE** Soft shades of caramel, cream, beige and taupe have been layered to create a neutral colour scheme that imparts a calm serenity to this inviting living space. Texture also plays a vital role, adding depth and definition, with accents of black and charcoal grey keeping the scheme firmly grounded.

**OPPOSITE PAGE** Simple panelled walls, stripped floorboards and an uncurtained window provide the perfect setting for Matthew Hilton's elegant yet contemporary Oscar sofa and create a look that is both humble and luxurious in this cosy nook. Original 1930s floral cotton cushions offer a vintage slant, while the squirrel cage lightbulb adds some stylish frugality.

*living*

A *Pale & Interesting* living room is all about real life. We all want a space where we can showcase our tastes and experiment with decorating ideas as well as a place to unwind away from the hustle and bustle of everyday life, but a living room must also be so much more than that.

Most living rooms these days have a multitude of tasks to perform, so if you want the end result to be successful, you need to give proper thought to your requirements and to how the room will be used. Will it be an adult-only zone, or will the

kids use it too? If so, make sure you plan plenty of storage for toys and computer games, and that the sofa has washable slipcovers. Do you need a desk in there? If that's the case, you might want to consider partitioning off an area so that whoever is using it can work undisturbed. Will you use the room for entertaining? Then make sure the furniture arrangement doesn't revolve entirely around the television. The secret is to strike the right balance between a relaxing retreat where you can put your feet up and unwind, and a functional, multi-tasking family room that will meet everyone's needs.

There are five main elements you need to consider when designing any interior: space, colour, line, form and texture. These are the fundamental building blocks of a room, shaping its look and feel. Unless you are designing and building your house from scratch, you will have to make the most of the space you've got. In general, larger rooms call for more substantial pieces of furniture, while a small room will need less bulky pieces with a lighter feel, to help maximize the space. However, rules are made to be broken, and you can have fun playing around with scale. One large piece of furniture can make a bold centrepiece in a smaller room, while massing together smaller items in larger rooms will add interest and texture. If your rooms are on the small side, then consider knocking a few walls through: open-plan living has a wonderfully relaxed feel that works perfectly in the *Pale & Interesting* home.

**ABOVE** A bold contrast between styles, ages and genres can be easily pulled together if you keep the backdrop clean and simple. Here, the sleek, contemporary lines of a B & B Italia sofa are highlighted by an ornate marble fireplace and the original decorative cornicing in this grand Victorian drawing room. A floorstanding lamp adds to the mix, as does the cushion made from a vintage 1960s silk scarf.

**RIGHT** A real home is one that allows everyday life to become part of the décor; where treasured possessions and personal touches are on show rather than hidden away. In this apartment in Sweden, a vintage Wurlitzer electric piano takes pride of place, with a wooden stool painted to look like a silver birch log offering somewhere to perch. A collection of black and white photos on the wall includes one of Bob Dylan by Barry Feinstein.

**THIS PAGE** Iconic retro classics combined with chain-store finds make for a relaxed and comfortable yet cool living room. White-painted floorboards and walls unify the eclectic mix, while huge windows flood the room with natural daylight to keep the overall feel bright and airy.

**THIS PAGE** With the help of some old metal trestles, reclaimed scaffolding boards are given a new lease of life as a side table that creates an essential focal point of texture and colour in this all-white room. The generous proportions of the squishy armchair plus a mohair throw add a note of luxurious comfort.

*Aim to contrast and complement textures throughout your interior, from walls and floors through to cushions and throws.*

When it comes to the arrangement of your space, the essential starting point is choosing a focal point. This will give the room a heart around which everything else revolves. A set of French doors with a view onto the garden, or a glazed armoire filled with elegant accessories are good examples of successful focal points. Alternatively, there is not much to beat the allure of an open fire or wood-burning stove. If your living room doesn't have a fireplace, consider having one fitted. There are plenty of specialist companies who can fit a steel flue and build a false chimney breast for you. A simple wooden frame around the aperture would suffice, but if you want to make a bigger statement, hunt down an antique mantelpiece. Don't worry if it has been sitting outside in a salvage yard for the last few years – if it has a weather-beaten surface, so much the better; it will add texture and interest to your interior.

**THIS PAGE** Gentle pastels, chalky greys and earthy neutrals soften the grandeur of this lofty space. Simple painted panels break up the vast expanse of the walls, helping to change the proportions of the room, while touches of vintage and retro style, and the contrast of luxurious and raw materials, help to dilute the opulence.

**FAR LEFT** Recycling with a touch of glamour. Here, a faded turquoise cushion, made from a pair of old embroidered satin curtains from the 1950s, adds a dash of colour to the dusky pink damask on this elegant daybed.

**LEFT** Mixing old and new. The flexible, fabric-covered flex from Helena Christensen's Flower lamp for Habitat has here been combined with a salvaged 1930s punched aluminium factory light shade to create something new and unique. The wall colour is Farrow & Ball's Hardwick White.

**BELOW** Modular seating is a boon; practical, versatile, comfortable and stylish, as demonstrated in this London family home. Covered in durable charcoal felt, this sofa looks smart and hardworking. The white leather Moroccan pouffe on the bare floorboards adds an ethnic twist that keeps the look relaxed and easy going.

Use your focal point as an anchor around which to arrange the sofa and armchairs, always keeping in mind the natural flow of traffic through the room, and the structure of the interior will soon start to take shape.

All rooms require a certain amount of empty or 'negative' space – the space around and between objects. Not only will this space give your furniture and accessories more impact and create a calm atmosphere but it will also create a feeling of depth. Depth adds a sense of perspective, which makes an interior lively and interesting. Secondary focal points are a great way to achieve depth. They are small vistas or vignettes that draw your eye through a room and reward it with something pleasant to rest on, thus helping to increase a sense of depth and space. A secondary focal point could be a sideboard just beyond the main seating area boasting an arrangement of glassware; or a vase of flowers on a console table behind a sofa. Mirrors are also a useful tool in the quest for depth – their reflections bounce light back into a room and create a feeling of extra space. Try grouping together a collection of decorative antique mirrors above a fireplace, or lean a huge floorstanding gilt mirror against the wall for a sense of casual elegance.

Colour is an essential tool. Choose gentle, soothing shades inspired by the natural world; off-whites, soft beiges, earthy neutrals and soft greys will create a tranquil effect, while gentle hints of colour such as soft pastels and muted vintage brights prevent an interior from looking washed out. For stronger

accents, try splashes of charcoal grey and indigo. If you are going for colour on the walls, keep furniture predominantly white for a light, fresh look. Conversely, white walls offer the perfect blank canvas for colourful furniture and accessories: a pebble-grey linen armchair, a soft green 1950s occasional table or a cushion covered in a pretty, original 1940s Sanderson floral pattern.

Walls and furniture contribute line and form. Tall vertical lines will create a sense of elegance and height – think of wooden panelling, spindly-legged chairs, tall cupboards or high-backed sofas. Horizontal lines have a more laid-back, relaxed feel. Achieve this effect by using items such as low-lying modular seating, a long, low shelf running the length of the room or squashy pouffes. As always, feel free to break the rules. One of the key elements of the *Pale & Interesting* look is contrast, so that the end result is balanced and harmonious.

Perhaps the most important piece of furniture you will need is a sofa. Comfort, practicality, durability and style are all essential characteristics of the perfect sofa, so take your time when shopping for a new one. Feather-wrapped foam seat cushions are an excellent option, as they give you the best of both worlds in terms of luxurious lounging and good support, plus you won't have to endlessly plump them up. A quality handmade sofa represents an enormous expenditure, so if

**THIS PAGE** The combination of relaxed comfort and formal display has made this eclectic room feel both grand and homely. Antique and vintage antlers adorn the walls, and an old wooden birdcage sits in front of the window. The cupboard in the corner by Dave Coote was made using salvaged doors that retain their original distressed paint finish.

**THIS PAGE** The ornate gilt mirror and twinkling chandelier are offset by rustic, almost monastic, elements in this Provençal home. The crisp white soft furnishings and contemporary standard lamp add a modern note, making this room an unusual spin on the French country theme.

**LEFT** Texture and colour play vital roles in any interior, giving it definition, depth and interest. The key to success is to contrast and blend the two elements to create balance and harmony. This charming wooden cabin demonstrates this in both its structural and decorative elements. The rough-hewn floorboards and whitewashed planking on the walls are combined with a set of huge, salvaged panelled doors painted a subtle shade of elephant grey. The daybed was constructed from two rusty, mismatched bed ends found in the garden, while the cushions and throw were made from antique linen sheets dyed a beautiful French grey colour.

**BELOW** A pile of miniature plaster casts makes an intriguing display atop a decorative pressed-glass cake stand.

your budget is tight and you are shopping at a chain store, consider getting an upholsterer to make you some feather-wrapped seat pads to replace the existing ones. Your sofa will feel like a custom-made model, but at a fraction of the price.

Coffee and side tables will also be on your essentials list, offering somewhere to place a cup, lamp or pile of magazines, as well as a chance to be a little creative. Try resting a couple of scaffolding boards on piles of bricks to make a low coffee table. You could fit castors or wheels onto an old architect's plan chest for an unusual yet very useful table, or mix up your look with the fluid lines of a retro Alvar Aalto moulded plywood piece.

A room devoid of texture will feel hard and cold, and what we are looking for is an inviting retreat that both soothes and feeds the senses. Aim to contrast and complement textures throughout your interior, from walls and floors through to cushions and throws. Tongue-and-groove panelling is a great way to add understated texture to walls. For something more unusual, try cladding one wall in planks of different widths and textures, then painting them all one colour for unity.

**THIS PAGE** Grey and white is a calm, soothing colour combination, and it doesn't have to feel cold or sombre. The addition of warm tones in the guise of a wooden bench and a row of bamboo stools ensures that this pale and elegant room is also cosy and inviting.

*Contrast and complement textures throughout your interior, from walls and floors to cushions and throws.*

**THIS PAGE** Freshly picked geraniums make a pretty display in this simple glass jar.

**OPPOSITE PAGE** The owners of this light and airy house on the South Coast of England have carefully retained the structure and form of the abandoned railways carriages around which it was built to create a home full of character and charm. The 18th-century Gustavian daybed covered in a vintage 1930s eiderdown offers a cosy corner for reading or contemplation.

If you have plain plastered walls, add texture with pictures or mirrors – cover a wall with framed black and white photos, perhaps. Wooden flooring can be rough or smooth depending on the type of wood and the finish. Bleached or white-painted boards bring a beachy feel, whereas reclaimed oak ones add earthy rustic charm.

When it comes to furniture and accessories, layer tactile fabrics such as chunky knitted throws, felted cushions and animal skins with antique linen curtains, battered leather armchairs and rusty metal tables. Then add decorative detail in the shape of twinkling glassware, cake stands piled high with corals or shells, glass cloches covering beachcombed fossils, mirrored glass votive holders or decorative plaster casts to complete the textural experience.

Once you have the look and feel of your living room covered, make sure the space meets all your needs. Plenty of storage for books, DVDs, CDs, computer games, the TV and the sound system will keep it clutter-free, while a variety of lighting options will guarantee that the room is versatile. Directional task lights, such as a classic anglepoise by a reading chair, are a must. A selection of side lights will allow you more control over light levels, and if you are fitting a chandelier, make sure it is on a dimmer switch.

**ABOVE** This bright, white beach house is the perfect example of relaxed open-plan living, where kitchen, eating and living areas all flow into each other to create one large open space. A couple of battered leather armchairs, an old trunk and mismatched dining chairs add to the uncontrived, laid-back feel. The collection of industrial lighting gives the room a utilitarian edge.

**LEFT** The classic combination of white and tan lends this rustic, wood-clad room a sophisticated air. A huge upholstered daybed offers the height of luxurious lounging, with a pile of fluffy blankets close at hand should the afternoon turn chilly.

**OPPOSITE PAGE** In an old factory that is now a family home in the South of France, the original stone fireplace and old wooden beams have been retained and carefully restored. The soft, neutral colour scheme provides a cool and inviting retreat from the punishing heat of the day, while plenty of natural textures ensure that the room feels warm and cosy during colder months.

**THIS PAGE** To make the most of the available light during the dark winter months, the owners of this country kitchen in a Swedish farmhouse have painted everything white. A huge wooden table dominates the room, and the butler's sink ties in perfectly with the country theme.

BLUR THE BOUNDARIES BETWEEN COOKING AND EATING TO CREATE A WARM AND WELCOMING SPACE THAT IS AT THE HEART OF THE HOME.

# cooking and eating

**THIS PAGE** Rows of open shelves make this light and airy kitchen space feel relaxed and informal. The freestanding island unit that houses the sink keeps the cook connected to the dining area while offering storage space and cleverly concealing potentially messy work areas.

**LEFT** An antique French hanging shelf left in its original, distressed grey paint finish offers a great alternative to wall-mounted cabinets and keeps the feel open and spacious. A piece of salvaged marble has been set into the wooden worktops to create a built-in pastry board.

**OPPOSITE PAGE** This pretty palette of pink and grey feels anything but sugary sweet, thanks to the simple, rustic nature of the rest of the room. An impressive collection of decorative English, French and Swedish porcelain can be admired through the glazed doors of the built-in cabinets, while an old metal filing trolley houses a library of cookery books.

**BELOW** Slim wooden batons painted white are an effective way to display a collection of decorative vintage plates. The walls are painted in Farrow & Ball's Pink Ground.

The kitchen is at the heart of the home. It is a place of nourishment, creativity and conversation where everyone tends to gather, lured by the promise of warmth and homeliness. The modern kitchen is a hive of activity that is no longer just a place for eating and preparing food but also a family room where everything from homework to hobbies to entertaining takes place. In order for your kitchen to be a hardworking, functional space, it needs to be an expression of your personality, both in terms of style and how you live, so defining these two elements is the first step in the creation of your culinary haven.

If you like a very sleek, ordered environment, a custom-made kitchen will suit you. However, if you veer towards a more relaxed atmosphere, then an 'unfitted' kitchen may be more appropriate. For those who are attracted to this casual style yet prefer the convenience of a fitted format, there are now many kitchen design companies who specialize in fusing the two. The materials you choose and the way you combine them will also have a huge impact on the look and feel of your space. A large expanse of stainless steel, for example, can feel cold or lifeless, but mix in some wood and stone and the finished result will be softer and homier.

*Give your table pride of place,
with plenty of space around it.*

**OPPOSITE PAGE** A truly individual mix of old, new and ethnic elements comes together to create a stylish ensemble in a Danish designer's family home. The high-gloss white-painted floors bounce the light around the room and pull together the disparate elements. Oversized fabric-covered hanging lights add a dash of tailored chic.

**FAR LEFT** A collection of 1960s transfer-print highball glasses brings colour and pattern.

**LEFT** Ice-cream pink rhododendrons make a pretty display in a simple, cream-coloured milk jug.

**BELOW** Wrap-around sash windows fill this bright, fresh dining room with masses of sunlight and offer amazing coastal views. White-soaped floorboards add to the all-white scheme while retaining the warm tones and textures of the natural wood. The oak table and chairs add a country vibe.

If, on the other hand, you have opted for a rustic all-wood style, then a few harder edges, such as a polished concrete floor or an aluminium splashback, will stop it from feeling too quaint. Whatever style you go for, the *Pale & Interesting* kitchen should be a light, airy place that is relaxed and welcoming.

Plenty of thought and analysis at the planning stage is essential if you want your kitchen to be not only aesthetically pleasing but also practical. The 'golden triangle' theory is a useful concept when designing a kitchen layout. The idea is to group together the three things you use the most – usually the sink, fridge and oven – so that they are within easy reach of one other. You may find you need a couple of work 'triangles', one that relates to cooking and the other to clearing up, in order that jobs like unloading the dishwasher and putting items away become quick and easy.

The placement of your oven and sink is another vital factor, as they are the two main fixed items in the room, and by making the most of their aspect you can create a striking focal point. A generous freestanding range-style oven or Aga has just the right good looks and no-nonsense practicality and will make a great centrepiece if set into a chimney breast. A butler's sink is a must. Functional, elegant and timeless, they work brilliantly with virtually any scheme, whether

contemporary or traditional, and come in a variety of sizes and styles to fit even the smallest kitchen. Showcase yours by placing it beneath a window and framing it with open shelves to create a built-in dresser effect.

In the kitchen, the single most important practical consideration is storage. The question of where to house everything needs careful planning, and making a list of all your kitchen paraphernalia is a good place to start. It will help you decide which items need to be stashed away and which you want out on show.

If you love entertaining, you may have lots of special equipment – a fish kettle, tagine or fondue set, for example. Do you use these items every day or only twice a year? How many sets of crockery do you own? Is there one for everyday use and another for special occasions only? How often do those special occasions come around? How much equipment needs to be close to hand, and what can be hidden away? Armed with this information, you will know exactly how much storage you need to create an uncluttered kitchen that works hard for you.

**ABOVE** A bunch of bay leaves has been hung up to dry under a wooden shelf. On top, a jar of shells sits alongside a ceramic head. The vintage school slate is a useful place to jot down a shopping list.

**RIGHT** A clever solution to the recycling problem. An antique French dolly tub has a specially made wooden lid and houses landfill rubbish, while an old metal pedal bin takes care of cans and bottles.

**OPPOSITE PAGE** The delicate palette of pale grey and white gives this light and airy dining space an almost ethereal feel. An old glazed cupboard shows off an impressive collection of white china and glassware, and a couple of slightly battered enamel shades add a touch of utility chic. Meanwhile, the mismatched selection of old church and quirky folding chairs lends the room an eclectic slant.

A soulless off-the-peg kitchen plucked straight off the showroom floor with endless rows of fitted cabinets is not right for the *Pale & Interesting* home. Instead, have fun and be creative, combining an antique dresser with industrial-style shelves or a sleek bank of fitted cupboards with a vintage French linen press. Scour salvage yards for inspirational finds such as old school lockers to house your mops and brooms, or a salvaged shop fitting that could be transformed into a kitchen island with plenty of storage space beneath. Mixing old with new in this way will add character and charm to your kitchen. Open shelves are a good option, as they double up as display space, allowing you to show off your favourite kitchenalia. Ask a carpenter to make wooden supports or source decorative cast-iron cistern brackets from a reclamation yard.

Kitchen islands are increasingly popular as they offer additional work, storage and seating space. A custom-built island can be home to a hob/cooktop or sink, but there are also plenty of options when it comes to recycled or ready-made versions. Old factory workbenches, stainless-steel

food prep counters from professional kitchen companies, plan chests or antique florist's tables would all work just as well.

Worksurfaces/countertops need to be hardworking. Honed Carrara marble, old wooden laboratory worktops or cast concrete all have just the right look. For a cost-effective option, use cheap, sustainably sourced floorboards and create an illusion of depth by fixing a skirt at the front, then paint them in hardwearing eggshell. You will need to repaint every now and then, but no more often than you would have

**LEFT AND OPPOSITE PAGE** Pewter has a wonderful soft bloom and steely grey hue. Here, a collection of antique pewter candlesticks creates a centrepiece on a rustic wooden table. An ornate gilt mirror in the distance adds formal glamour to this simple room, with its bare floorboards, rough plastered walls and table made from a discarded metal workbench.

**ABOVE** An imposing 18th-century Gustavian armoire with raised reed panelled doors, still boasting its original grey paint, houses glassware, china, crockery and cutlery in this Swedish dining room.

**OPPOSITE PAGE** This kitchen is the perfect demonstration of how texture can bring depth and interest to an all-white scheme. A gnarled and warped butcher's block takes centre stage, bringing an earthy and rustic element to this simple space. The reflective surfaces of the glazed tiles and the extra-wide Aga bounce light around the room while also acting as a foil to the rough, reclaimed oak worksurfaces and cast-concrete units. Exposed rafters on the ceiling and plain painted floorboards keep the look relaxed and easy going.

**ABOVE LEFT** Butler's sinks have timeless appeal. Chunky, classic, practical and enduringly versatile, they fit into both modern and traditional kitchens, as demonstrated here, where this generous example ties in with both the vintage-style tiles and the rustic, limewashed units. The all-white scheme unifies the different elements, pulling together the wide range of materials that has been used.

**ABOVE** Old French coffee bowls and hand-thrown rice bowls from the Far East are stacked side by side on an open shelf.

to oil a hardwood surface. Splashbacks should follow the same principle: tongue-and-groove panelling, sheets of zinc and simple glazed brick tiles (or square ones set on the diagonal) all combine practicality with utilitarian chic.

If you have inherited a kitchen that you can't afford to replace, then a simple revamp may be all that is needed. Changing or painting cabinet doors can transform the look and feel of tired units. Playing around with the size and arrangement of the doors is a clever way to break up the standard proportions associated with off-the-shelf kitchens. Try replacing single doors with split ones for a more cottagey feel,

or remove doors and hinges altogether, sliding baskets onto internal shelves for a rustic look. If you hanker after an open-plan space but knocking down walls is out of the question, what about installing a hatch between two rooms? Make sure the aperture is a generous size and frame it with a plain, flat architrave, and there will be no danger of it looking dated or old fashioned.

Mundane practical details should not be overlooked. Get on top of recycling with colour-coded bins and source appliances that are hardwearing and energy efficient. Freestanding American-style side-by-side

**OPPOSITE PAGE** A warm palette of whites, greys and neutrals lends this outdoor kitchen a rustic charm. Simple white cushions have been made to fit each of the vintage Pauchard Tolix stools, while a long runner made from antique handwoven hemp and two outsized wooden candlesticks bring a luxurious feel, ensuring that, despite its basic qualities, the space feels both elegant and homely.

**RIGHT** Mismatched chairs painted different colours add to the friendly informality of this cosy family kitchen. Practical wood worksurfaces, bare boards and chunky kitchen cabinets make the space practical and hardworking. Vintage china contributes to the retro theme, and huge double doors onto the garden flood the room with natural light.

refrigerators look fantastic, as do the prettily coloured retro-style fridges available. Taps/faucets need to be both sturdy and stylish; old hospital-style ones are ideal, but if ever there was a time to go for reproduction over reclaim, this is it – there is nothing charming about a leaky tap/faucet.

A kitchen colour scheme should be clean and simple, and make the most of any natural daylight. Introduce doses of stronger colour by subtle means, such as painting the inside of a glazed cupboard in a delicate china blue. Alternatively, leave it

to your accessories to do the job for you. Vintage kitchen utensils, storage tins, bread bins and china often come in gorgeous muted pastels, as do many modern appliances.

A dining table is a major investment. Choose one as large and as sturdy as your space and budget will allow. Old trestle or refectory tables are tough enough to take all the abuse a busy family can throw at them, and big enough to handle any amount of multi-tasking. They also blend perfectly with just about any scheme, whether it is modern or traditional. Give your table pride of place, with plenty of space around it to allow guests to push back their chairs for relaxed after-dinner conversation. A jug of flowers is all that is needed to adorn it for everyday use, but when entertaining, get out the antique table linen and group twinkling glass votive holders around silver candlesticks. Keep floral displays low so that they don't block your guests' view. Start a collection of patterned vintage china and create a harlequin effect with mismatching dinner and side plates. Don't worry if your seating doesn't match; an eclectic mix of chairs and benches will only add to the relaxed effect. And if you have space in your kitchen, a sofa is the pièce de résistance, offering your guests somewhere to retire to after dinner. Choose a casual, informal style with loose slipcovers that can be thrown in the machine – that way, no-one feels that they have to be on their best behaviour!

**ABOVE** An old enamel teapot, a blue and white china jug and an antique Moroccan milk bottle create an unusual collection on a high shelf that runs along under the eaves.

**LEFT** Vintage pastry utensils, spatulas, palette knives and food moulds have been mounted in simple shadowbox frames to create a trio of charming pictures in this wood-clad kitchen by the sea.

**OPPOSITE PAGE** A clever mix of rustic, industrial, seaside and vintage elements gives this light and airy interior a *Pale & Interesting* look. The white-painted horizontal wood planking on the walls and the simple cabinets create a blank canvas for touches of blue, orange and grey, while the white-soaped floorboards retain the wood's natural surface texture and pattern. The simple blinds have been made from antique narrow-loom hemp.

**THIS PAGE** This fresh and pretty Shaker-style bedroom is the perfect mix of elegance, prettiness and pared-back simplicity. Fitted cupboards provide plenty of storage space, enabling the owners to keep the room clutter-free, while the delicate duck-egg blue shade softens the scheme, dispelling any ideas that blue is too cold or clinical for a bedroom.

THE BEDROOM SHOULD OFFER
A CALM, PEACEFUL RETREAT AWAY
FROM THE HUSTLE AND BUSTLE
OF YOUR BUSY DAY.

# sleeping

**THIS PAGE** A set of reclaimed antique French
shutters has been ingeniously fashioned into
a bedhead in this light and airy beach-house
bedroom. On the wall, an old metal jelly
mould has been converted into a lampshade
and casually hung from a hook, continuing
the recycling theme.

A bedroom should offer the perfect balance between indulgence and simplicity: a peaceful retreat of gentle, sleep-inducing shades, simple furniture, soft bedding and a few decorative touches to keep it personal. Light, muted colours help create a tranquil mood, so in the bedroom the *Pale & Interesting* palette really comes into its own.

Analysing what makes you feel relaxed and comfortable will help you to create the perfect boudoir. Do you like sleeping in a pared-back, almost monastic space, free from clutter or knick-knacks, or do you prefer a prettier, more feminine style, where vintage prints combine with painted furniture for a cosy environment? If you tend to sleep better on

holiday, you could conjure up the atmosphere of a Greek villa with whitewashed walls and touches of Aegean blue, or a romantic Caribbean clapboard house decorated in chalky pastels.

There are many ways of introducing colour into your bedroom: bed linen, curtains, a rug or even a pretty 1930s dress casually hung on the back of the door, but if you are going for colour on the walls, make sure it is subtle rather than overpowering. Soft greys, pale lilacs and pinks, the gentlest aquamarine or creamy neutrals will all hit the right note. Floors should be simple and unfussy. Stripped or painted floorboards are ideal, as they look clean and simple but feel soft underfoot.

**THIS PAGE** Mixing up styles and genres is a great way to create a personal feel, as shown in this serene bedroom where minimalism, rustic charm, faded grandeur and modern design have all been boldly thrown together. A baroque-style antique carved wooden bedhead, stripped of its upholstery, shows how to give a contemporary treatment to an old piece.

**ABOVE** Contrast is a key element in the *Pale & Interesting* home. In this pared-back bedroom, where exposed beams and bare floorboards tell a story of rustic simplicity, the gilt finishes of an ornate 18th-century mirror and a Louis XV-style chair strike a note of opulence and glamour. A beautiful silk dress offsets the delicate reed panelling of the antique Swedish armoire.

The bed is the most important piece of furniture in the room. Cast-iron bedsteads are an ideal choice, as they lend an air of both romance and austerity – an important consideration in the *Pale & Interesting* home, where contrast is a key element. There are plenty of reproductions around, but original antique beds often have more intricate detailing. Don't be put off by the fact that they are not available in standard double sizes either – specialist companies can now extend bedframes so that they can accommodate modern king-size and super king-size mattresses.

An old French wooden bed will lend a touch of glamour, but you will need to temper its highly decorative qualities to keep the feel of the room understated. You can do this by making the rest of the room very simple, or you could re-style the bed by stripping out the caning and retaining the bare frame, or reupholstering it in thick canvas or linen.

**ABOVE RIGHT** Grey is a soothing colour that is ideal for creating a calm feel. The important thing is to pick a warm shade and add plenty of white accents, to keep the room light and fresh. In this minimalist interior, the warmth of the reclaimed wood floor adds extra depth to the scheme, while a curtain hanging beside the bed softens the monastic frugality.

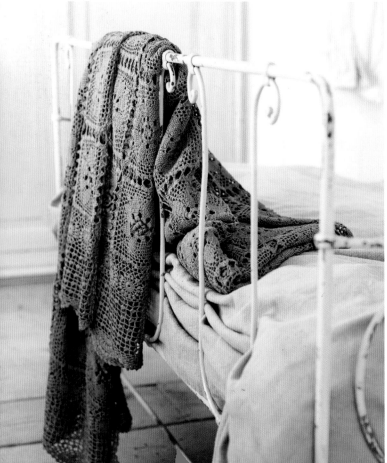

**ABOVE LEFT** Simple and effective: a pretty crochet-covered hanger hangs from a humble wooden peg that has been plugged straight into the tongue-and-groove panelling.

**LEFT** Fabric dye is a brilliant way to refresh tired or out-of-date bedding. The vintage crocheted bedspread and duvet cover in this rustic cabin were dyed using Dylon's Antique Grey. It is interesting to note how different materials take dye in a different way – both of these items were dyed in the same vat using the same colour.

**ABOVE AND OPPOSITE PAGE** A decorative Victorian iron bedstead takes centre stage in this romantic bedroom. Diaphanous cotton muslin curtains dyed a gentle shade of lilac inject a shot of pretty colour that is echoed in the delicate pastel hues of the framed sea anemones hanging on the wall. A pair of salvaged antique shutters, with their original paint finish intact, introduce texture and interest to the plain white walls, while a pair of chunky sawn logs act as bedside tables and add a rustic texture. An embroidered antique linen sheet acts as a simple bedspread.

*Soothing colours and tactile fabrics will help turn your space into a relaxing retreat where you can put your feet up and unwind.*

**THIS PAGE** A retro clock sits on a vintage mirror bedside table designed and made by Dave Coote. The glass lamp base is from Eastern Europe, dating from the 1950s or '60s.

**THIS PAGE** A classical toile de Jouy design has been revived in a fresh new colourway in this stunning wallpaper by Manuel Canovas at Colefax and Fowler. White curtains and bed linen keep the room light and fresh, while the plastic 1960s light and the antique Venetian mirror contrast to great effect to create a lively and interesting scheme.

If you are going for the mattress, divan and bedhead option, make sure that the base is on legs, as this will stop it looking too much like a solid block and will create a feeling of space. Once you have decided on your bed, spend some time researching mattresses. It is well worth investing in the finest-quality mattress you can afford, as the average person is said to spend a third of their life asleep.

When it comes to bedside tables, be imaginative. A wooden stool, an old zinc dolly tub turned upside down or a simple block of wood will suffice, as long as it is big enough to hold a book and a glass of water. If you have chosen a traditional-style bed, contrast it with something sleek and modern like a Perspex cube. A recycled metal factory trolley will strike an industrial note, or lift a monochrome scheme with a touch of pastel colour in the shape of a 1950s-style spindly-legged side table.

Storage is a fundamental concern. Use alcoves to house custom-built closets, or create a whole wall of storage reusing old shutters as cupboard doors. Antique armoires, linen

**THIS PAGE** Pale grey walls and white floorboards keep this generously proportioned bedroom light and airy while also providing a clean backdrop for darker items such as the Victorian chest of drawers and the vintage floral eiderdown. Old shirt boxes offer extra storage under the bed, and an antique wooden sea chest under the window houses spare bedding.

**ABOVE** A collection of vintage hatboxes provides extra storage in this elegant bedroom. The handsome battleship-grey wardrobe has been given a feminine and slightly edgy touch with the addition of the hot pink tape that picks out the panelling on the doors, while a simple country rocking chair introduces just a hint of rustic charm.

presses and chests of drawers are all great options too, and should provide enough space to house the average-sized wardrobe. However, if space is short, or you are a clothes addict, squeeze in extra storage wherever you can. Push baskets under the bed or build a slim cupboard on the landing to house shoes and bags. In a spare room, fix a hanging shelf with hooks so that guests have a place to hang their belongings.

Window treatments should be light and airy. Shutters are a good choice, as they block out early morning sunshine while keeping the warmth in during the winter months. Floaty muslin or lightweight linen curtains will make the most of natural daylight and diffuse the room with a soft glow. Antique linen sheets make no-sew instant curtains when hung from a simple pole using café clips. Hunt out sheets with delicate threadwork so that the light can filter through the decorative designs.

**ABOVE RIGHT** The all-white colour scheme in this pretty beach-house bedroom makes the most of the beautiful seaside light, and square-edge wooden planking, as opposed to tongue-and-groove panelling, helps to keep the overall feel contemporary. Touches of soft pastels add femininity and banish any sense of starkness.

**BELOW** A collection of salvaged shutters makes an unusual bedhead in this small, simple bedroom. An antique French shelf provides some storage and hanging space, while the dainty crystal chandelier adds sparkle. Crisp white bed linen and a vintage floral eiderdown look fresh and inviting.

**RIGHT** The panelled doors of this built-in wardrobe have been extended to create a bedhead effect that frames this low-level divan and mattress, also creating

a handy narrow shelf that holds books, a glass of water and a few carefully chosen treasures.

**OPPOSITE PAGE** A set of reclaimed doors, resplendent in their original soft green paint finish, has become the focal point in this simple rustic cabin and brings a touch of elegance to an otherwise basic interior. The antique metal fold-up bed is dressed in old French linen dyed grey, and a discarded axle stand has been fashioned into a novel bedside table.

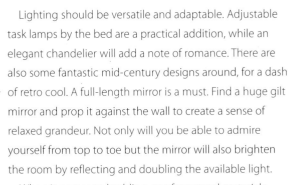

Lighting should be versatile and adaptable. Adjustable task lamps by the bed are a practical addition, while an elegant chandelier will add a note of romance. There are also some fantastic mid-century designs around, for a dash of retro cool. A full-length mirror is a must. Find a huge gilt mirror and prop it against the wall to create a sense of relaxed grandeur. Not only will you be able to admire yourself from top to toe but the mirror will also brighten the room by reflecting and doubling the available light.

When it comes to bedding, opt for natural materials. Crisp cotton and crumpled linen feel good against the skin and will keep you warm in the cold months and cool when it is hot. Take a cue from the fashion world, layering patterns and textures and mixing old with new. In winter, combine brushed cotton sheets and woollen blankets with thick quilts and vintage eiderdowns. In summer, keep it simple with cellular blankets, crocheted bedspreads and antique linen sheets.

Decorative touches are best when they double up as storage or display opportunities for your treasures. Think of box frames holding a vintage beaded evening bag, a pair of favourite shoes out on display, a dish piled high with pretty bracelets, a gorgeous dressing gown hanging from a peg or a pile of colourful hatboxes stacked on the floor.

**THIS PAGE** A rich variety of textures can transform a bathroom into a sensual haven of relaxation. Here, the dusty finish of a polished concrete sink unit is combined with a fossil, a soapstone dish and a distressed mirror.

**OPPOSITE PAGE** A claw-foot cast-iron bathtub has been painted a gentle blue in this tranquil wooden-clad bathroom. The pipes for the wall-mounted taps/faucets have been boxed in, creating a simple shelf.

MIX CONTRASTING STYLES, TEXTURES AND MATERIALS FOR A BATHROOM THAT COMBINES LUXURIOUS SENSUALITY AND UNFUSSY FUNCTIONALITY.

*washing*

**THIS PAGE** In this simple cabin, a set of antique panelled doors hides a tiny ensuite bathroom lined with galvanized sheeting. A salvaged steel bath fits snugly into the small space, and the simple, inexpensive hardware-store taps/faucets have been mounted onto a block of wood.

The last few decades have seen a revolution in the way we perceive and use our bathrooms. Gone are the days when the bathroom was regarded as just a clinical, utilitarian cube for our daily ablutions. It is now considered a relaxing sanctuary, somewhere you can shut yourself off from the rest of the household and indulge yourself guilt-free, whether it be for a five-minute power shower or an hour-long soak in a tub full of bubbles.

Once upon a time the bathroom was often relegated to the smallest room in the house, but these days it is not uncommon for a spare room to be converted into a large bathroom, reflecting our changing attitudes to this once-neglected room. The *Pale & Interesting* bathroom should be the perfect combination of luxurious sensuality and unfussy functionality; a light, airy place that is clutter-free but never cold or unwelcoming. Avoid the obvious and rethink your approach to decorating your bathroom, choosing contrasting styles, materials and textures. Forget matching suites and floor-to-ceiling tiles. Instead, pair rough wood with smooth marble, an Art Deco basin with a sleek

**LEFT** A contemporary square sink sits atop a weathered old wooden table to create an usual bathroom vanity unit. The silver-leaf mirror on the wall echoes the dull sheen of the elegant brushed-nickel taps/faucets, while the large wicker basket in the background holds linen waiting to be washed.

**ABOVE** The cast-concrete bathtub and sink unit were custom-made for this atmospheric bathroom reminiscent of a Turkish hammam. The chalky finish of the cast concrete has a tactile, sensual quality that softens the hard edges and makes this space feel like a luxury spa.

modern bath, shiny ceramics with bare plaster walls or sparkling mirrors with rustic baskets.

The bathtub will be the most important element in your self-indulgent oasis. Roll-top tubs are the ultimate in luxury. There are plenty of lightweight reproduction models available that are perfect if you are worried about how much weight your rafters can take (a cast-iron bath full of water weighs a huge amount), but be warned: their shiny newness can look a little glitzy. If possible, hunt out an old bathtub from a salvage yard or antique bathroom specialist. Old tubs

come in all sizes and shapes, and double-ended, coffin or slipper designs will make a stunning statement in any bathroom. If a decorative cast-iron bathtub isn't your style, then consider old copper or steel versions, or even a cast-concrete design. They are more comfortable than they look and hold the water temperature beautifully.

Think carefully about the positioning of your bathtub. A freestanding model in the middle of the room has a wonderfully decadent feel. Alternatively, put it under a window so that you can enjoy the view while splashing in the tub.

**ABOVE** A vintage pressed-glass jelly mould holds a selection of handmade soaps.

**RIGHT** By painting the walls and all the architectural details the same colour, the owners of this spacious bathroom have created a calm, composed feel. Darker accents have been introduced in the form of the radiator, blind and flooring to add depth and definition to the scheme. Old weighing scales stand in the corner.

**THIS PAGE** A controlled approach ensures that this elegant bathroom, in a sympathetically restored Georgian house, feels soothing and peaceful. Oversized panelling forms the backdrop to a double-ended roll-top tub while also creating a narrow shelf that holds pictures. An Art Deco clock adds a retro touch and the slate tiles on the floor are practical and hardworking. The chunky woven basket holding discarded towels provides some rustic texture.

SILENCE PLEASE

Your basin doesn't have to match your bath – go for an elegant mismatch. A sleek modern design would be the perfect foil for an ornate roll-top bathtub, but if the other elements in your scheme are already streamlined and contemporary, take the opportunity to introduce something different. A small butler's sink on an old wooden table or a shallow bowl-like basin on a metal French café table converted into a washstand would both add charm and individuality.

There is nothing better than a walk-in shower. Make sure the cubicle is roomy enough to allow you to bend over without hitting your head on the side and that you don't feel claustrophobic when you close the door. If space is at a premium, the alternative is a wet room where your shower

**THIS PAGE AND OPPOSITE** A cast-iron bath takes centre stage in a lofty bathroom flooded with natural daylight. A fruit picker's ladder is in use as a towel rail, painted in Farrow & Ball's Lamp Room Gray to match the bathtub. An old wicker basket housing fresh towels sits in the fireplace, and a collection of Victorian engraved mirrors on the wall encircles an early 19th-century tin clock.

**BELOW** A custom-made cast-concrete unit houses a pair of sinks in this simple yet glamorous washroom. Copper piping has been fashioned into minimalist taps/faucets, and a strip of wavy-edged lead forms a splashback. The antique crystal chandelier and matching sconce and the carved wood mirror add decoration and pull the interior back from austerity. The low concrete wall just seen to one side conceals a walk-in shower.

doesn't need to be enclosed. In a small bathroom, fit a shower over the bath. An antique linen sheet hung from a simple tension wire will make an ideal shower curtain. Back it in plastic or try waterproofing it using one of the off-the-shelf solutions available nowadays.

Bathroom accessories need attention too. Choose honest, hardworking designs that are more about function than style, and don't feel you have to box in your pipework either – as long as you get your plumber to use chrome or copper, it will just add to the no-nonsense utilitarian feel.

The colour scheme in your private spa should be soothing and gentle. Lots of white with touches of faded blue or aqua will create a clean, fresh feel, while earthy colours reminiscent of a wintry beach scene, such as sandy beiges and cool greys, will have a restful effect. Walls are the obvious vehicles for introducing colour and also offer the chance to bring texture into a scheme. Mosaic tiles in pastel shades of turquoise or peppermint green create the retro look and feel of an old public baths, whereas wooden cladding will create a warmer atmosphere. For an unusual effect, explore the possibilities of galvanized steel sheeting as a wall covering, or track down some old American embossed metal ceiling tiles and give them a new life as a splashback. Plaster is an incredibly versatile material and particularly suited to the bathroom if you opt for a Venetian marmorino or traditional Moroccan finish, both of which have waterproof qualities. Made from crushed marble and lime putty, they are expensive and labour intensive, but the end result will be well worth it. Floors should be practical and non-slip. Rough-hewn wooden floorboards, poured concrete or slate all have a homespun effect entirely in keeping with the *Pale & Interesting* style.

If you want to maintain a sense of calm serenity in your bathroom, good storage is indispensable. A custom-built cabinet fitted into an alcove will provide plenty of storage. Another idea is to fix a shelf in front of the window and use it to hold toiletries decanted into pretty glass bottles so that the light can shine through them. Don't pass up the opportunity to bring some recycled features into your bathroom. Old tea trolleys, luggage racks, salvaged factory shelving or a chest of drawers are all good choices. Old wire baskets can hold a pile of toilet rolls, while wooden

**THIS PAGE** Wood cladding ensures that this bathroom feels warm and cosy despite its simplicity. An Edwardian toilet and cistern have been painted a soft shade of grey and a fishing weight dangles from the end of the flush pull. A scaled-down butler's sink takes on a contemporary feel on top of a custom-made vanity unit.

**THIS PAGE** A standard tub is mounted below a teak surround and boxed in with wooden planking in this fresh, beach house-style bathroom. Shelves at one end create plenty of storage space for bathroom essentials such as bath salts, shampoo, good reading material and, of course, a radio.

**THIS PAGE** The clever design of this bathroom maximizes space by combining the structure of the cast-concrete bath with an open shower. Piles of fluffy white towels are kept close at hand in a chunky woven basket, and a simple wooden stool offers a place to perch.

crates make a great alternative to plastic storage boxes. Fruit-picker's ladders can also be pressed into service as bath racks or towel rails. Leave them untreated or paint them in a soft shade that complements your scheme.

Lighting should be no-nonsense and, of course, observe all the safety guidelines. Aluminium bulkhead fittings have a nautical feel, while a pressed-glass pendant light (choose one specified for bathrooms) will add a vintage French edge. Electric chandeliers are not suitable for bathrooms, but if you have your heart set on the twinkle of crystal drops, you could hang one that holds candles. Nothing beats bathing by candlelight.

Little details are important. Pile fluffy cotton towels in baskets and hang textured honeycomb hand towels from decorative hooks. Fill antique glass apothecary jars with cotton wool or scented bath salts, and use vintage teacups or saucers as charming alternative soap dishes.

**THIS PAGE** A home office should be a relaxed, personal space, somewhere both inspiring and organized. In this sunny study, a tall metal cabinet provides plenty of filing space, while the comfy armchair offers a welcome change of scene after long stints on the computer.

# *working*

PRACTICALITY, COMFORT AND INDIVIDUALITY
ARE THE ESSENTIAL ELEMENTS OF A WORKSPACE
THAT IS BOTH EFFICIENT AND INSPIRING.

**THIS PAGE** Reclaimed scaffolding boards and
a piece of salvaged marble are supported by
decorative iron cistern brackets, creating a row
of shelves that house plaster-cast moulds in
this artist's workshop. Dust sheets are kept close
to hand in an old metal bath beneath.

**THIS PAGE** Files and books are hidden away behind black and white toile de Jouy curtains in this elegant office, where modern technology sits side by side with antiques.

**LEFT** Botanical studies are pinned up alongside children's drawings in a home office.

**BELOW RIGHT** If space is at a premium, consider creating a home office in the garden, like this charming writer's retreat in a shepherd's hut. A small wooden table provides enough space for pen and paper, while an old machinist's chair is practical and stylish. The tiny wood-burning stove was custom-made by a local blacksmith, keeping the space cosy whatever the weather. A panel of corrugated iron protects the wood-clad walls from the heat of the stove.

**THIS PAGE** An old kitchen table in bubblegum pink adds a refreshing shot of colour to an all-white workspace. A wood and metal task lamp adds a masculine note.

With technology advancing at breakneck speed and new gadgets being introduced on a monthly basis, the way we work and the face of our workspaces is changing rapidly. Once a static, fixed location, these days an office can be anywhere that you lay your wireless laptop or check your multimedia phone. But whether you run your business from home, or simply need somewhere to pay the bills and write emails or just do a bit of sewing, a room of one's own is a luxury that is well worth indulging in.

When it comes to creating a home workspace, discard any notions of trying to recreate the bland efficiency of the corporate environment. The beauty of a work area at home is that you can be your own boss and create a room that is personal, productive and inspiring.

Deciding where to position your creative haven is your first step. In an ideal world, you would be able to dedicate a whole room to the purpose, allowing you to spread out and get on with business, free of any distractions or disturbance from the rest of the household.

In reality, we don't all have this luxury. In many homes, studies double up as guest rooms. If this is your situation, a sofabed is a space-saving option, as well as providing you with somewhere for an afternoon power nap. If space is at a premium, incorporate a workspace into your living room or kitchen/diner, stowing office files and paperwork away in an old linen press or a funky retro sideboard. An old tin tea caddy or antique box can hold pens, pencil sharpeners and other office paraphernalia.

Choosing a colour scheme for a home office is an important consideration, as different colours can have different effects on your stress, energy and concentration levels. In general, cool muted shades tend to calm the nerves, aid focus and increase a sense of space, while warmer shades and brighter colours stimulate and energize. Somewhere in the middle is probably the best option, so go for light, neutral walls and floors, and add touches of stronger colour in the form of accessories or furniture. A study with white walls could be tempered with neutral accents in the shape of a battered leather armchair, whereas a serene, dove-grey room could be sharpened up with red-striped linen blinds and an office chair covered in pistachio-green linen.

The desk should be as large as your space will allow. Vintage steel desks have a great utilitarian look, but they are quite collectable now and tend to come at a high price. For a cheaper alternative, go for a wooden desktop on a pair of trestles, which

**ABOVE** A sturdy trestle table of chunky proportions creates a generous working space in this simple study in Provence. Floor-to-ceiling cubbyhole shelves allow plenty of room for books, files and decorative objects.

**LEFT** Paintings, studies and works in progress by the artist Peter Oswald adorn the walls of this charming studio. Old metal stacking boxes provide ample storage space for artist's materials and an old battered cupboard has been revived using old linen to line the doors.

**OPPOSITE PAGE** In this light and airy painter's retreat in the South of France, a simple tabletop sits atop a pair of metal trestles and provides plenty of space for jars and pots filled with paints, brushes and drawing utensils. A polished concrete floor is cool and practical in a warm climate, while the freestanding shelving holds stacks of sketchbooks, paper and other artist's essentials.

**OPPOSITE PAGE** Salvaged floorboards, complete with paint splatters and the decoration of the house from which they were taken, have been used to cover a wall in this rustic cabin that acts as a designer's studio. Old office pigeonholes hold paper, drawing materials and tools, while a simple enamel gas stove brought back from Greece is used to make those all-important cups of tea. The unusual stove is a converted honey spinner – the original inner cage now sits alongside, holding logs.

**RIGHT** A huge enamelled old factory light hangs from an antique winch to create a home-made rise-and-fall pendant light in this interior design studio. A wide workbench provides plenty of space for laying out fabric samples or large plans.

come in a huge variety of designs for all tastes and budgets. A workbench and stool is a great option in craft rooms. Look out for old factory or catering benches, or construct a space-saving bench using old planks and cast-iron brackets from your local salvage yard. You may even be able to fit two work areas into the same room, one for your computer and paperwork and another for more hands-on work.

A good-quality office chair is a wise investment. Twentieth-century classics are on many people's wish lists, but there are other vintage office chairs around that may not have the same iconic status, but make up for it with comfort, good looks and affordability. Trawl eBay and second-hand office furniture shops, or visit one of the many specialist retro furniture companies. Another option is to buy a new chair and transform it with a slipcover in cotton canvas or a pretty vintage floral.

A sturdy, directional task lamp such as a classic anglepoise is all that is needed to light your desk. Pens, pencils and paintbrushes will sit happily in an old jug or glass jar, while letters, bills and other bits of paper can be piled into flat baskets and wooden trays stacked neatly on the desktop.

MAKE COMFORT AND
PRACTICALITY A PRIORITY
TO ENSURE THAT YOUR
OUTSIDE SPACE IS LAID BACK
AND WELCOMING.

*outside*

**THIS PAGE** A white-painted Adirondack chair sits on a deck made from reclaimed scaffolding outside a weatherboarded beach house. Hydrangeas and lavender complement the silvery grey of the old metal buckets and dolly tubs in which they are planted.

**OPPOSITE PAGE** Creating an outdoor room is a great way to maximize use of your outdoor space. Here, bamboo sofas and armchairs, piled high with soft squabs and scatter cushions, have been arranged to create an inviting alfresco sitting area.

**OPPOSITE PAGE** A cosy retreat that doubles as a guest room has been created at the bottom of this London garden, where it soaks up the last rays of the evening sun. The window was salvaged from a reclamation yard.

**FAR LEFT** The Antelope chair by Ernest Race usually has a wooden seat, but this unusual pair with metal seats make ideal garden chairs. Painted grey, they are in contrast to the background of white weatherboarding.

**LEFT** Smoky faceted glass tumblers have been pressed into service as tealight holders on a Moroccan metal tray.

**BELOW** A simple summerhouse provides an idyllic hideaway in this Swedish garden, allowing the owners to make the most of their outdoor space during the unpredictable summer weather. The black and white scheme employs gingham and toile de Jouy plus antique furniture to create an air of classic elegance.

Treat your outside space in much the same way that you do the rest of your home. Designers talk about bringing the outside in, but it works the other way round too. Whether you have rolling acres, a small yard or just a balcony, it should be an inviting extension of your interior.

When it comes to furniture, make comfort your priority. Create an outdoor seating area that is every bit as cosy and welcoming as your indoor one. Make wicker sofas plump and inviting with cushions, pile up blankets for chilly evenings, hang a candle chandelier from a tree and use pieces of log as side tables or extra seating. Invest in a brazier and light a welcoming log fire. Drape outdoor lights (you can get solar-powered ones) in a tree and invest in glass storm lanterns for when the evening sets in.

If you live in an area with an unpredictable climate or you need shade from the sun, then a verandah, porch or gazebo will protect furniture from the elements. Building a wooden structure may be beyond your budget or space allowance, in which case rig up an awning using sailcloth. Keep it taut with guy ropes attached to metal eyelets. If your taste leans towards a more contemporary look, build an outside banquette seating area using sleepers (get a wood yard to cut them for you) for a chunky modernist feel. Cushions and rugs will soften the seating and can be stowed away indoors during winter months.